The Ring and the Cross

By Barbara Rogers

A Novel of the Dark Ages

The Ring and the Cross: A Novel of the Dark Ages
By Barbara Rogers

ISBN 978-0-9834956-2-8
Library of Congress PLN: 2011930890
All rights reserved

No part of this book may be used or reproduced, stored in or introduced into a retrieval system, or transmitted in any form, or by any means (electronic or mechanical, photocopying, recording, or otherwise), without the prior written permission of the author, except in the case of brief quotations embedded in critical articles or reviews. The scanning, uploading and distribution of this book via the Internet or any other means without the permission of the author is illegal and punishable by law.

For permission to quote from this book, address your inquiry to:

SpiritBooks LLC
wilson@spiritbooks.me

For more information: www.spiritbooks.me

1. Venantius Fortunatus 2. Sixth-century France 3. Late Roman Empire 4. St. Gregory of Tours 5. St. Radegund of Poitiers 6. Merovingian Kings 7. Christian Church History 8. Christian historical novel

Printed in the United States of America by LightningSource, Inc.

Cover design by Jeffery Shirley

Copyright © 2011.
First Edition 2011

For the Gary and Darielle
Richards Family

Table of Contents

A Historical Foreword……………………………....1

Map of Merovingian Gaul………………………3

Merovingian Genealogy……………………....…4

Historical Characters……………….…………....5

Prologue The Sage: Boëthius ……...…….…....7

Book I   The Poet: Venantius Fortunatus……....19

Book II The Warrior: Brunhild……………..…..79

Book III The Saint: Radegund……………..……135

Epilogue: The Letter of Fortunatus…..............185

Historical Afterword……………………..…….190

Historical Events………………………..…....194

Bibliography……………………………..…....195

Study Questions for Group Discussion……...196

A Historical Foreword

Sixth-century Europe has often been seen as the ugliest, most brutal age in that continent's history, a time of regression, decay, and collapse. It was all those things, but it was also the place and time when the next age of civilization, the Christian Middle Ages, was being born. Birth is not only a triumph of nature, but a painful and messy affair. Merovingian Gaul was wracked by currency inflation, civil war, church-state conflicts, violence, and promiscuity, along with ignorance of manners, civic responsibility, and letters on the part of immigrating hordes.

The world that saw the birth of Venantius Fortunatus, poet and adventurer, was neither Christian nor pagan. Italy had become a land dominated by barbarians, swarming with fiercely mustachioed Lombards who stampeded their way to power wherever Roman troops collapsed. Thanks to the bubonic plague, the empire was twenty-five million people fewer than it had been in 500 AD, and the Roman army had lost two-thirds of its strength. Wages and prices had been frozen in the vain hope of keeping inflation under control. Light-weight gold coins were minted, bloating the currency. The barbarians continued to pour south and west, fleeing pressure from Asian hordes in the east.

By the ruinous 540s, when Venantius Fortunatus was a child, Emperor Justinian slackened his grip on the dying West and turned his face eastward toward Jerusalem. Taxes increased to feed his armies and construct his buildings. The balance of power in what had been the Roman Empire was shifted to the East. With the death of the barbarian king Theodoric in Italy, two years after he had murdered the philosopher Boëthius, the western empire was finished. Only in the newly Christian Frankish lands that would someday be France and in Visigothic Spain, was a glimmer left of what had been Rome. Something of the old Rome remained, however. The savage Merovingian age, from 500-750 AD, was at the same time a period in which Christian saints built monasteries that sowed the learning, polity, and social order of the feudal age.

Out of the monastic schools came the teachers and sages who mined Roman classics and transformed them into medieval philosophic and poetic texts. From the cathedral schools arose the great European universities in the eleventh century, while the arts of illuminated manuscripts and religious sculpture prepared the way for the twelfth-century artistic and literary Renaissance. From the Latin poems of Fortunatus addressed to his beloved patroness, Queen Radegund, grew the eleventh-century love songs of the French troubadours to their unattainable ladies. The new spiritual age flowered in a radically new soil, watered with the blood of martyrs and tended by saints in their monastic gardens. The impetus to Roman achievement was imperial glory; the impetus to Christian culture was the glory of God. What the sixth-century Christians had to do in their violent time, as we try to do in ours, is to seed the future with what we know is true: that love is the tropism bending us away from ego, toward God.

Map of Merovingian Gaul

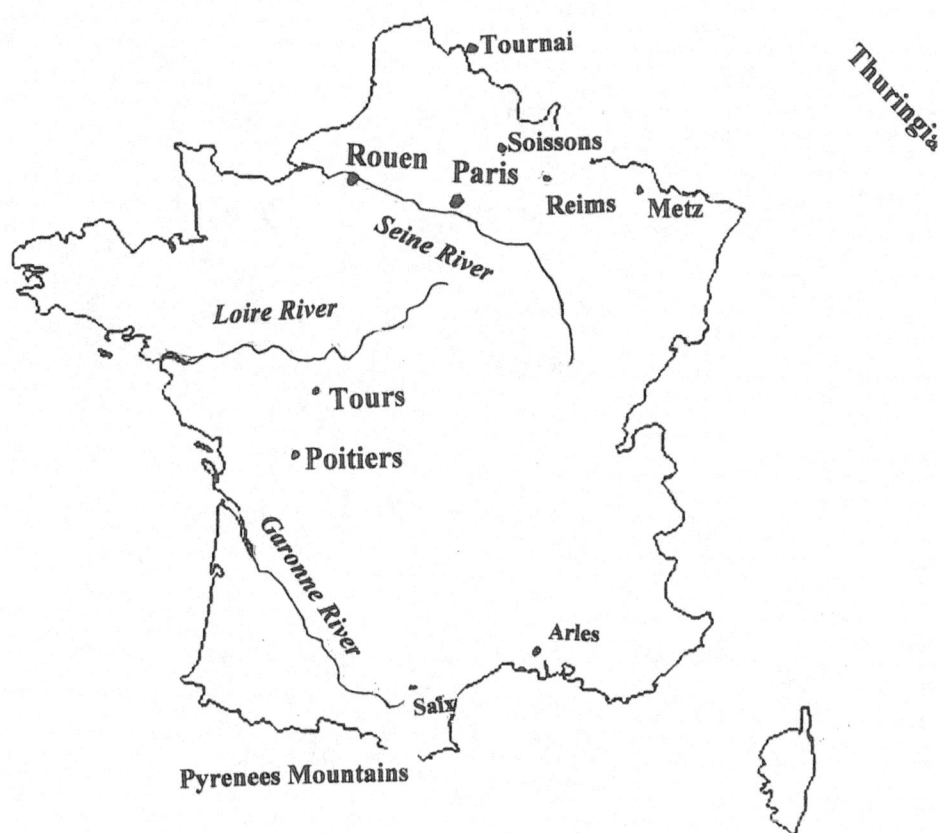

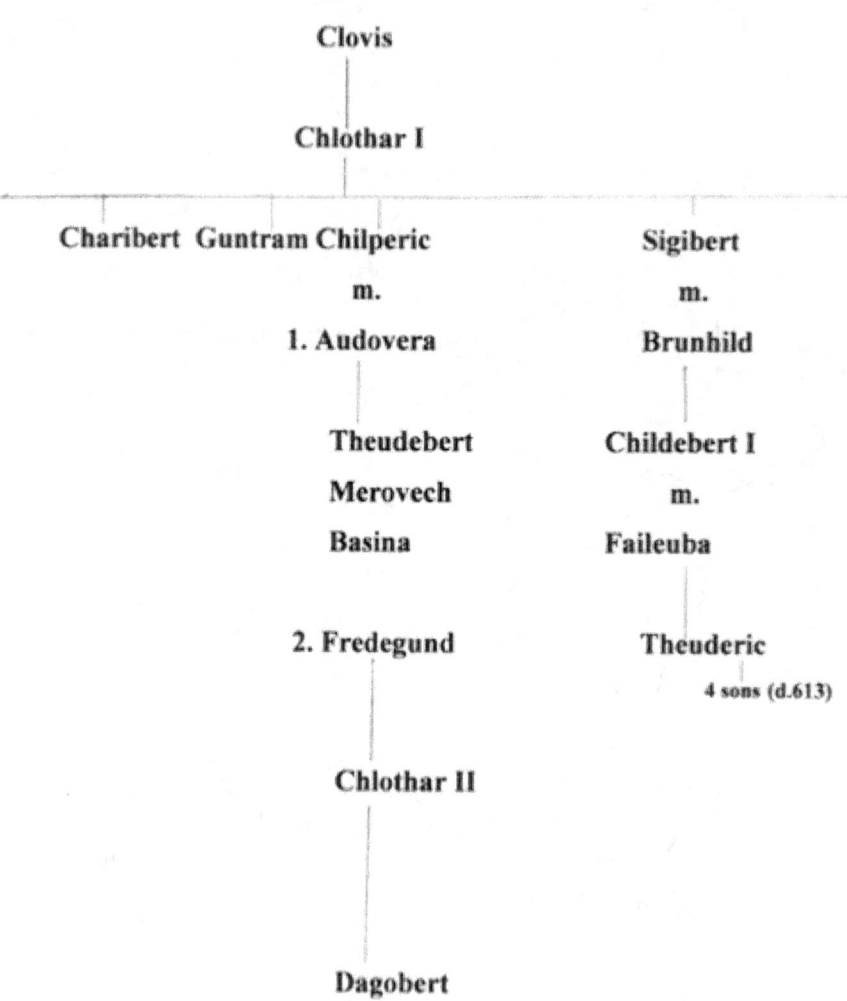

Historical Characters

Agnes   (birth and death dates unknown) Abbess of Holy Cross Monastery

Athanagild Visigothic king of Spain, father of Princess Brunhild

Boëthius (d. 524) Roman statesman, author of *The Consolation of Philosophy*

Brunhild (d. 613) Queen of Francia, Wife of King Sigibert, mother of Childebert II

Childebert II (d. 595) Son of Sigibert and Brunhild, King of Francia 592-5

Chilperic (d. 584) Son of Chlothar, King of the Franks in Neustria

Chlothar I (d. 561) Son of Clovis (d. 511) and heir to all Francia

Chlothar II (d. 629) Son of Chilperic by Fredegund; King of Francia

Chlothild Daughter of Charibert, Nun at Abbey of the Holy Cross

Fortunatus (birth date uncertain, d. early 600s) Poet and later Bishop of Poitiers

Fredegund (d. 597) Wife of Chilperic, mother of Chlothar II

Galswinth (d. 567) Elder daughter of Athanagild king of Spain, wife of Chilperic

Gogo (d. 581) Aide to King Sigibert and tutor of King Childebert II

Gregory (d. 591) Bishop of Tours (575), author of *History of the Franks*

Guntram (d. 593) Son of Chlothar I, King of Burgundy

Hermanfred (d. 531) Uncle of Radegund, Usurper of Berthar's throne

Justinian (d. 565) Emperor of the Eastern Roman Empire, husband of Theodora

Merovech d. (578) Son of Chilperic by Audovera, 2nd husband of Brunhild

Praetextatus (d. 586) Bishop of Rouen, god-father of Chilperic's son Merovech

Rauching, (d. 587)   Powerful Austrasian duke, enemy of Brunhild

Radegund (d. 587) Princess of Thuringia, wife of King Chlothar I

Rusticiana (dates unknown) wife of Boëthius

Sigibert (d. 575) King of Austrasia, Son of Chlothar I, husband of Brunhild

Theodoric (d. 526) Visigothic King of Italy

*Do not deceive yourselves. . .the wisdom
of this world is foolishness with God.
I Corinthians 3:18-19*

Prologue
The Sage
Boëthius

524 A.D.

"I want that traitor dead," cried King Theodoric, spittle flying from his lips. "Boëthius has been a thorn in my flesh for too long." The king's face contorted as if the thorn had pierced his vitals as well. "To think I loved him once and made him second only to myself."

His attendant, the Mayor of the Palace, did not say what he was thinking, that Boëthius was second to no one as a scholar, a Christian, and a statesman. Once he was gone, they would not see his like again. Probably King Theodoric would be just as glad for that, since lately he had gotten the notion that Boëthius wanted his throne. The king had become so rabid that no one could reason with him, even over as preposterous an opinion as this one. *Perhaps Theodoric has a demon eating at his soul*, the Mayor thought, *but a king is accountable to no one, certainly not to me.*

"Shall I order beheading for him?" The king's Mayor of the Palace did not dare change his expression as he wiped his face.

"Something slower. The man plotted to bring me down," Theodoric snapped, fingers drumming on the arm of his throne. His nails were bitten to the quick. "Boëthius will be an example of the way I deal with traitors."

The Mayor sighed. Over the years, the king's judgment had eroded as his power had grown. His eyesight was failing too, and he could see well only when he stood close to what he looked at. His world was shrinking around him and with it his once-keen vision of the larger picture. Since he could not see what was on the horizon, he tended to assume danger on all sides. Theodoric now seemed afraid of everyone, though he might better have feared himself and his downhill slide into madness.

"Besides," Theodoric fretted, trying to find a less ignoble reason for his hatred of the great sage, "Boëthius thinks Jesus was more than a man. A heretic consul is an insult to our Arian faith."

The Mayor nodded. "I understand, majesty, but the informers who malign Boëthius. . .do you think they might have reason to lie? Jealousy, perhaps? He's always served you well." The Mayor backed away a little, since he could sense that violence was about to erupt. It would not be the first time. "Boëthius is not an Arian Christian like us, to be sure. Still. . ."

Theodoric drained his large, ornately wrought gold cup and threw it across the room. "Boëthius is too smart for his own good or mine," Theodoric shouted, his voice cracking as if he were about to break down in tears. "Yes, once I treated the man like my own brother. In those days, we tried to make old Rome rise again. Now that dream is dead."

"But the people admire Boëthius." The Mayor knew he was pushing his luck, but his respect for the sage pricked his conscience. "They believe he is the last great Roman among us. If you execute him, might they not say that you used your left hand to cut off your right?"

Theodoric pounded the table next to him, spilling a tall silver ewer onto its side. Red wine flowed across the white marble table top and spattered one sleeve of the king's long, purple-edged tunic.

"I grow tired of hearing this traitor praised for his learning and his manners. These Romans are all alike, looking down on us Goths as if we were vermin. Boëthius and his kind must be taught a lesson."

Ah, now we hear the real reason, the Mayor thought. *There is no arguing with shame.* Not wanting to earn the painful fate that the philosopher had brought upon himself, the Mayor bowed his way out of the room, one fist over his heart in an obedient salute. Boëthius was already a dead man, and with him, the Roman culture that had existed for a thousand years. The Mayor grieved for that extinction, but not enough to ensure his own ruin by further disputing the matter.

Outside the throne room, the Mayor found Rusticiana, the wife of Boëthius, who awaited word of her husband's fate. She was a woman of noble proportions, her arms full and round, her forehead high, and her long, white wool mantle flowing down to her sturdy ankles. A thick, silver-laced black braid was wound around her head like a crown. Rusticiana's dark eyes were red-rimmed, and she wiped them with the backs of her hands. *She cares nothing for fine manners now,* thought the Mayor. He felt a pang of sympathy, imagining his own wife in such straits. This woman's father had been a wealthy senator, and she had inherited his fortune. Because all assets belonged to the husband, that fortune would now be confiscated by the king. The loss of her inheritance, he knew, was not the reason this woman was weeping. She was one of those rare wives who had chosen her husband for love.

"What did he say?" Rusticiana put one damp hand on the Mayor's arm. "Did you convince him that my husband is innocent?"

"I tried, but the king is determined to make an example of him."

"He's already an example," she retorted. "An example of excellence. What's the king's objection to that?"

"Madam, you don't understand." The Mayor bowed slightly. "In these times, excellence is dangerous. A man who rises above the common herd is bound to be resented. I heard one of the king's *comitates* say, 'Boëthius talks too good. He makes me feel dumb.' The king feels much the same way. There you have it."

Rusticiana shook her head. "My husband's genius helped Theodoric build a kingdom. Let me go in and remind this ungrateful king why Emperor Justinian isn't ruler here instead of him."

She tried to push past the Mayor, who gently blocked her way. "You mustn't go in there, my lady. The king's in one of his fits. Just now, he would kill you along with Boëthius."

"You think I care to live?" Rusticiana managed to get one hand on the heavy, ornately carved door. "Without my husband?"

She slid between the Mayor and the door, leaning her whole body against it as she lifted the lever holding it in place.

"No, madam, give it up," the Mayor cried, trying to grab her arm but seizing only her mantle. "You can't do any good here."

As Rusticiana entered the throne room, her mantle fell away, and she stood before the king in her simple, Greek-style gown. The patterned red border of her skirt fluttered in the breeze from the open window. At first, Theodoric could not see who she was, so she moved closer to him.

"You're too late, Rusticiana," Theodoric said, once he had recognized her face among the vague, shifting colors that comprised his failing sight. "I've sent the order for your husband's execution. You'd do well to go home and pack what you need to take into exile."

Rusticiana tore at her hair, scattering bone hairpins on the floor. Her long nails drew blood on one cheek. "Kill me instead of him," she cried. "You know Boëthius. If I died in his place, he would think it a worse punishment than if he were killed himself."

Theodoric squinted as he tried to bring her face into focus. "That may well be true, but my councilors would not be satisfied. They want the kingdom governed only by Goths. Boëthius is not one of us."

"Certainly not one of *them*, your majesty," Rusticiana replied, trying to keep her voice low. "His goodness shames them. His wisdom makes them feel stupid. That's his only crime."

Theodoric turned away from her, pausing at a curtained doorway behind his throne. "Your husband's crime is being a man in a time when wild beasts rule the world. Haven't you heard him say as much? My informants have."

Rusticiana lost control and shouted at Theodoric. "Your informants! Little men with little minds. Boëthius made you a great king. You owe him something for that."

"So I do." As he disappeared behind the gold-embroidered curtain, the king gestured to the Mayor of the palace. "See to it that Rusticiana and her sons keep one estate, something up in the northern hills, where they won't be noticed. Now, go away, both of you. I'm late for my nap."

Boëthius sat in a prison cell, awaiting execution. He knew the king had been jealous of him for a long time, envying his way of being right, no matter what the issue. *I never thought to end my days in jail. It's too soon*, Boëthius mourned in his cold, dirty cell. He had only begun his grand project: to translate all the Greek philosophers into Latin and leave their wisdom for those who survived the swallowing of civilization by hungry barbarian hordes. As he had written to Rusticiana's learned father, "There's no point in writing for the masses, since no one but you knows what I'm talking about." He made little headway in his task before he realized that preserving the past was less important than shaping the future. *The body of Rome is past saving*, he told himself, *but perhaps there is hope for its soul.*

In creating the *Consolation*, Boëthius did not address the Christian God, but Lady Philosophia, a wisdom figure not identifiable with any faith. He had modeled her on his wife, who had always seemed to him as much goddess as woman. Since he had entered her father's household as an orphan, she had loved him like a sister. Then, when they were older, she had loved him in a new way, surprising them both with her passion. Her father let them be married, young as they were. His judgment, as always, was not mistaken. Their marriage had been like that described by Scripture between Christ and his Church, and it had borne good fruit.

Like so many educated men of his time, Boëthius kept one foot in the classics and one in Christianity, living uneasily in two conflicting worlds. He himself was a blend of both—a philosopher in the Neo-platonic tradition and a Roman politician. Not only was he a consul, but his two young sons were also. Service to a barbarian king would exact a high cost, as Boëthius had long feared. He was well aware that the family glory was unlikely to last.

Now he was preparing himself for death by torture, thanks to the suspicions of Theodoric, who had, some years back, praised the sage for his musicianship. The king had even asked Boëthius to choose a skilled harp player to entertain the king of the Franks, who had requested such an artist. Boëthius complied, but raised one refined eyebrow in surprise at the thought of a brawling Germanic chief wanting a harp at his banquet table. Perhaps, he thought, the king's wife had suggested the harpist, since she was from the still-Roman south of Francia and a Christian, unlike the Frankish king. The queen might well wish for gentle music to soothe her savage pagan mate. That harp might have worked its magic after all, since Clovis, the Frankish king, had turned Catholic in the year 511, unifying Francia with the Roman faith. *Perhaps*, the sage thought, *Rome's future lies with the northern tribes. Who would have guessed that the men we hired as our mercenaries would end by being also the protectors of our faith and culture?*

A thin-faced man with graying hair and a straight, grave mouth, Boëthius looked much like the ancient senators whose busts lined the colonnade at the center of his villa. *They are all dead now, as I soon will be,* Boëthius reflected. At forty-five he was as old as most people ever got. Even without the death sentence upon him, Boëthius had run out of time to complete his task. *All your actions,* he read silently from his manuscript, *are done before the eyes of a Judge who sees everything.* He wrote these last lines as the sun went down over the red-tiled rooftops of Pavia, a once-beautiful city that was now a mere quarry for scavengers seeking cut stone. It occurred to him that he, too, was somewhat of a scavenger, mining the classics for what he might be able to offer future ages, bereft of learning as they were likely to be. He had hoped the Lady Philosophia would console him in his eclipse, but now had his doubts. To his visionary goddess of wisdom, he had poured out his misery at being punished for the good he had done, but she spoke to him no more.

What use has it been to save my noble friends from losing their wealth and their lives? Boëthius asked himself. The senators whom he had protected from the barbarian king were letting him rot in jail, while lying informers poisoned the ears of King Theodoric with made-up tales of Boëthius's ambition and treachery. Ultimately, Boëthius had to conclude, the philosophic man had to surrender to the flow of history and fate.

The coming of the immigrants from the harsh north to the depopulated, inviting Mediterranean lands had been inevitable, Boëthius knew. Still, their invasion had been a tragedy for its destruction of *Romanitas,* that grand idea of civic order that had shaped an empire.

In the end, he had a few friends and students who cared enough to brave the contagion of his disfavor with the king by visiting his prison cell. One by one, they came and went, their voices hollow as those of Job's friends in the Jewish Bible and as comfortless. *My fantasy of the tattered but beautiful Lady Philosophia was more satisfying,* Boëthius reflected. But he put on a cheerful face, not wanting his image to suffer in the eyes of those who honored him and the tradition he taught by his words and his life.

He had trained his followers in the thought of Pythagoras, who had, a thousand years before, seen the universe as absolute harmony, a great ring of light gathering all existence into itself. On this vision early astronomers modeled the crystalline spheres that circled the earth and made the heavens sing. Honoring the teachings of Pythagoras, Boëthius wore the ancient master's gold ring which had been handed down through intervening ages as a sign that power and wisdom could work together for human good. The heroes of antiquity had worn it—Plato, Aristotle, Alexander the Great. For Boëthius, the ring was a reminder that wisdom remained even when powerful empires collapsed.

As he looked at the ring, he felt the spirit of Pythagoras come over him, and prayed that in the face of death, he would not prove unworthy of the master who once had sung the praise of wisdom. It was music, Pythagoras taught, that reshaped the disordered, earthbound human soul into the image of divinity. It was music that drew together matter, mind, and God into one cosmic chord. Following his master's example, Boëthius himself often played the Greek lyre. He felt like Orpheus ready to enter Hades and to bring the soul-illumined world of archaic Greece back to his darkening age.

As had Orpheus and Pythagoras, Boëthius reluctantly accepted the idea that love could never be perfectly embodied in earthly experience, though he had tried to celebrate this wedding in his own with Rusticiana. Even that marriage, close as it came to heaven, could not replicate the harmony he knew was possible between matter and spirit. The two could be linked by analogy—as above, so below—and in the act of art. But only in Christ, the incarnate God, did Boëthius find them perfectly united, a single rainbow in a continuum of dissolving colors.

He grew tired of explaining his vision to his followers, but tried one last time. "The body is like musical sound, vibrating to the energies that shape its form. You can't separate the body from the music that makes it dance. Creation happens through the Incarnate Word resonating in space. That is what I believe."

His visitors bowed their heads in silence. They had no need to speak, since they believed as their master did. Boëthius turned as if listening to a faint, far-off voice.

"Go, my friends, so you won't share in my disgrace. My wife is coming, and we need to be alone."

Rusticiana paused at the door, waiting until the visiting disciples left. Then she entered and held out her arms to her husband. At first, they said nothing to each other, but only stood close together, so that their two shadows merged into one.

"I went to Theodoric," she said, her voice breaking as she spoke. "He thought to buy me off with one of our estates in the hills."

"Take the offer and go. You and our sons will need some refuge in the storm I see coming. Without me, Theodoric will certainly antagonize Justinian and bring the might of Byzantium down on this wretched kingdom. Hide on your hilltop, my dear, and tend your garden. I will die more easily knowing you are safe."

Rusticiana hid her face against his shoulder. "I would rather die at your side."

"But I would rather you didn't," Boëthius smiled, lifting her face to his, one finger under her chin. "Let us save what we can, especially my writings. They are the best of me."

"No amount of scribbling can equal what you are. I will live only to honor your memory." Covering her face with her hands, Rusticiana sat down on the hard bench that served her husband as a bed.

Boëthius seated himself beside her. "Don't despair. While you live, I live too. And we will meet again in God. You know that."

"But Theodoric means to torture you," Rusticiana said, her voice muffled against his shoulder. "I've brought you hemlock. Would you take it and die an easy death?"

"I must accept the cross I'm given. Your father raised me to be a Roman stoic, and your mother taught me to be a Christian. Neither would countenance suicide. Nor can I."

Boëthius was determined not to break under torture. Theodoric, whom he had served so honestly and well, would not have that satisfaction. Regardless of the pain he suffered, Boëthius intended not to lose command of his soul. He would hear the music of the turning cosmic spheres as he died. Or so he hoped. Rusticiana knew better than to argue with her husband. She poured wine for him from the flask hanging at her side and offered it to him ceremoniously, as if it were the communion cup.

"I never thought to be in the garden of Gethsemane myself," Boëthius said, setting down, untasted, the Falernian wine she handed him. "Yet here I am. God's will be done, not mine."

The cup containing the wine was made of poorly-fired clay, marred by ridges and pockmarks. Boëthius ran his fingers over the rough surface of the cup and sighed, remembering the crystal Alexandrian goblets at his home, where his wife would sit this night, grieving at her lonely table. He had always hoped to provide her with security and surround her with beauty. Perhaps, he thought, he had been too preoccupied with Lady Philosophia to realize he was putting his wife in danger. Only God knew what would become of her and their two sons, now that his fortune and favor with the king were gone. Friends had promised to take care of the family, but they might falter, if Theodoric threatened them. His gently-reared sons were likely to fall apart if life turned hard, as life had a way of doing.

"I have nothing left but the sacred ring of Pythagoras," Boëthius said. "Theodoric took everything else. All that I valued as a Roman, all that I tried to rescue for those who will come after us is gone. Or soon will be. This ring handed down from our master has brought me wisdom, but not power."

Boëthius held up his right hand that wore the ancient gold ring. He surveyed it with regret, unwilling to show such pessimism, but unable to help it. The threat of imminent torture and death did not, after all, encourage good humor.

Pulling the ring from his finger, Boëthius said, "Take it, my dear. Give this talisman from the past to the newborn son of my student, Fortunatus. May it bring the child more joy than it has me."

Rusticiana took the ring, still warm from her husband's flesh, and held it to her heart. "Marcellus Fortunatus says he will raise his little Venantius to love the classics and follow your example."

"Poor boy, then," Boëthius said, tying up the last of his scrolls and handing over to his wife the bundle containing all his wisdom. "He'll have to make sense of living by spirit in an age that lives only by the sword. I could not. It would be kinder to raise him as an oaf."

Placing the ring on her finger, Rusticiana studied it. The gold looked as if it had been woven from two strands, then fused together in a white heat. A diamond was wrapped between the gold threads. "Where did Pythagoras get such a ring, do you think?"

"It is said that the old northern gods made it to give man something of divinity, hoping that wisdom and power would grow together like the strands of gold in the ring. So Pythagoras taught."

Boëthius reached out and touched the circle of gold one last time. "I think of this ring as a symbol of the ancient culture we have lost." The sage smiled a little, his lips hardly moving. "Now we must find our unity and purpose not in the state but in the Church, the Body of Christ. The alternative is unthinkable—every man for himself, the way of the barbarians. Chaos."

Rusticiana carefully poured the wine Boëthius had not drunk into the flask she wore at her side. Nothing of value would be wasted, if she could help it. She would keep what she could of the goodness God had given the world and pass it on.

Footsteps echoed in the stone halls of the prison, and Boëthius tried not to shudder at the sound. "I hear my jailers coming. You had best leave or be taken away with me. Theodoric has become a madman who thinks everyone is after his throne. God knows I am not, but Theodoric is not in touch with God."

Boëthius held her briefly, laying his cheek against hers. "Our times may be dark," he said. "But in the end, my love, there will be light. Hold that hope."

Silently, Rusticiana bowed to him as if he were an emperor. She left the cell without looking back, not letting her husband see her tears.

Boëthius sat still as footsteps pounded on the stone pavement and the barred door burst open. Three men entered, preceded by their smell, and the fastidious sage winced. The men had knives in their belts, but as soldiers, looked like a bad joke. Their tunics were ragged and their breastplates dented. Grinning with embarrassment and meanness, they clasped chains around the wrists of Boethius and dragged him away.

"My Lord and my God," Boëthius whispered as he fell to the floor, scraping the skin off his knees. "I follow you not willingly, but I follow."

As she lingered at the prison gate, Rusticiana could hear her husband screaming for a merciful death and knew that Theodoric's torturers would not grant it. It was said they planned to bind and tighten a cord around the sage's head until his eyes burst from their sockets. Rusticiana shuddered as if it were she the soldiers were torturing. She leaned against the stone wall for a moment, trying to choke down the sobs that rose in her throat. Her husband was gone, but she and his followers would not forget him.

"Kyrie eleison," Rusticiana prayed out loud, her voice shaking. "Christ have mercy. Lord have mercy on him. On us all."

The flask of fine wine bounced against her side as she ran from the place where Boëthius, the last Roman, was dying. A light was going out, leaving the world in darkness so deep that men forgot the sun and stumbled in the shadows of Plato's cave, not even knowing what they had lost.

> *For the good that I would, I do not.*
> *But the evil which I would not, that I do...*
> *O wretched man that I am, who shall deliver me*
> *from the body of this death?*
> *Romans 7:19*

Book I
The Poet
Fortunatus

565 AD

"You should come with us to Greece," Phoebe said, standing close to their ten-year-old daughter, Agnes. "Emperor Justin will never find you, if we hide among the city crowds."

"The emperor already has spies on my trail," Venantius Fortunatus said, looking away from them and out the window. The tile rooftops of Ravenna had always fascinated him, though now his failing eyesight seldom allowed him to enjoy their rippling symmetry. The roofs varied in height so that they looked like a red sea as they flowed into the distance. Beyond them was the Adriatic, on which Phoebe and Agnes would soon be sailing.

"In Constantinople, I would be an easy target for the emperor. No, Phoebe, I'm going north into the Frankish forests." As he said the words, he felt charged with the adventure of it all, anxious to be alone and on his way.

"Can't we go with you?" Phoebe's round brown eyes filled with tears. "Your mother would never know."

"My mother knows everything." Fortunatus almost believed that. His mother had long since found out about Agnes, the child he had fathered at sixteen. Phoebe, her Greek slave, had been sent away pregnant, and had lived for years with a friend on the outskirts of Ravenna. Still, Phoebe had managed to sneak off to meet her lover, which his mother also knew, having her spies.

"Now that you expect another child, you wouldn't be safe travelling into the wilderness with me." Fortunatus sighed as he pulled Phoebe's arms from around his neck. "No, you must go back to Greece, a free woman. With the gold I'm giving you, your life should be an easy one."

Agnes said nothing, only looked at her father intently as if trying to read his mind and heart. She was not pretty like her mother, but her gentleness made her comfortable to be with, though not just now. Fortunatus turned away, not wanting to see the sorrow in her small, olive-colored face. Sometimes failing sight had its advantages. *She knows I've made a mess of things, and will someday hate me for it. My sins be not upon her, O God.* Fortunatus vaguely wished he had spent more time with the child, more than a few clandestine visits, but now it was too late.

He sent her, her mother, and the unborn child away on their sailing ship, knowing he was a coward, and worse, knowing he had chosen the way easiest for him. So he had always chosen, and no doubt would go on choosing, if his mother was right. And of course, she always was. Living away from her would be a test for the young poet, one he meant not to fail, blind or not. He could play his harp without seeing, Fortunatus thought, trying to cheer himself, and poetry came to him as easily as breath. *Still, the beauty of women, the sunrise over the water, friends sitting around a hearth-fire, these I will miss when my eyes give out. O God, if you forgive my sins, grant me my sight again.* A rush of warmth and optimism swept through him, and for a moment he thought he was healed. *But miracles,* he reflected, on noting that his eyes saw no better than before, *miracles are not for the likes of me. I've never felt sorry enough to stop sinning, only sorry I was caught.* His heart heavy more with regret than contrition, Fortunatus made his way home, his staff tapping ahead of him to test the way.

Young Venantius Fortunatus had written a long poem in fine classical Latin recounting the career of Emperor Justinian's wife, Theodora, in all its seamy detail. Now Justinian was dead, and Theodora's nephew, Justin, was on the throne, ready as his uncle had been to exact vengeance on the fellow who had insulted his empress-aunt. Fortunatus had a bounty on his head and no choice but flight.

He did not want to leave his beloved Ravenna, on the eastern coast of Italy, where he lived the sweet life, enjoying his noble mother's fine house. He loved Ravenna, with its theaters and baths, its fine architecture and witty company. The city had not always been so grand. Long before Venice was founded in 558, fisherman had set up their flimsy shacks over pilings on the swampy isle that became the city of Ravenna, during Justinian's era a center for collecting imperial taxes. In earlier times, the marshes were drained and canals were built to make the growing commercial city a harbor for the Roman fleet. Ravenna became a cultural center where literary men like Fortunatus wrote and declaimed their work. Artists flocked into town and were given materials for their art. In return, they created mosaic panels that would crumble only with the solid stone that bore them. Fortunatus longed to create poetry that would live as long as these mosaics, but wondered who would read it.

The great tradition is gone, he thought. *No use trying to bring it back* He had not followed the advice of his father, a simple man, obedient to authority. The elder Fortunatus had tried to carry on the teachings of his great mentor, Boëthius, but had died when his son was barely out of his teens. Something had passed between them of the great philosopher and his belief in a love that might be embodied in both human flesh and nature. It was at least a hope, though nothing like faith. Fortunatus had inherited the manuscripts of

Boëthius, but faith was not a thing that could be passed from father to child. Some essential luminosity had left the world with the death of Boëthius, his father had believed, but had not the words or wisdom to say what it was.

So little time, thought Fortunatus, as he hastily packed his leather bag, with Boëthius's *Consolation of Philosophy* at the bottom, protected by a few writing implements, blank Egyptian papyri, and a single change of clothing. *Life is more fragile than a flower stretching open in the springtime sun*, Fortunatus reflected, looking out the window behind the great house, onto a garden colored by wildflowers waving cheerfully in the breeze. It annoyed him that nature was not cooperating with his elegiac mood. He sighed, remembering Phoebe and Agnes waving to him until their ship shrank to nothing and was out of sight.

The poet's sin with Phoebe was doubtless the reason for his growing blindness, railed his mother. Fortunatus believed his weakening sight was more likely the result of too much reading, though he prayed uneasily for healing from the local saint Venantius and for the son he would never see. His father had always told him that someday he would raise his own son in the tradition of classical Rome, but his son, if son it was, would be raised without him.

Phoebe, carrying most of Fortunatus's gold along with his unborn baby, had promised to send their children to a school that taught the ancient classics. No other coin but gold would be useful, Fortunatus knew, since inflation had been growing at a monstrous rate, despite the reforms of Diocletian, three hundred years before. Sensible people had long since turned to bartering goods and services. Better that Phoebe should go back to Constantinople, where she could raise the children in civilized comfort. She also promised to teach the new child Greek, which Agnes had already begun to learn. In that respect, at least, the children would be better than their father. Fortunatus had been too lazy to learn Greek, to his father's distress, but had made up for his deficiency with a near-perfect command of classical Latin. So that his children would someday read the work of Boëthius and perhaps follow in the great man's footsteps, Fortunatus had copied out the the sage's discourse *On the Trinity* and sent it with Phoebe in the bag of gold coins. Which of the two would prove to be more valuable, Fortunatus did not know.

The poet was aware that he had not kept faith with the ideals of his Pythagorean forebears and that he cared more for a drinking song than for the music of the spheres. His father, had he lived, would be ashamed of his son, who regardless of his fine classical diction would sooner drink with his artist friends than pray. Fortunatus was glad he did not have to explain to his father that Lady Philosophia had never spoken a word to him and that he cared little she had not. Philosophy, from his point of view, made men nothing but trouble. *Prayer to St. Venantius was likely to do more for my healing and my children than any amount of advice from Lady Philosophia,* he thought. *Much good she did poor Boëthius in his last miserable hours.*

It was not to philosophy that Fortunatus looked for help, but to his friends. As soon as he learned that the new young emperor in Constantinople wanted him dead, he wrote to his childhood friend, Bishop Vitale, who came at once to Ravenna. The young bishop was planning to stay in the city only overnight before resuming his journey north. He, too, was on the run from the new Emperor, whose wily general Narses had recently conquered Vitale's episcopal seat and had orders to instate a bishop favorable to Constantinople, not Rome.

Vitale and Fortunatus had been friends since childhood, though one, the devout Vitale, had gone into the clergy, and the other had become a partying poet. They sat in the *cucina* of Fortunatus's home, watching his mother's servants prepare a rabbit stew for dinner and weighing the poet's options. The young bishop urged Fortunatus not to consider travel for its own sake, but to go where divine grace led him. Vitale drank water, while Fortunatus emptied several cups of wine, each time fumbling for his drink, seeing only a blur on the long wooden table.

"I curse this blindness," he muttered. "How can I travel? How can I write? God ought better to have taken my life."

"Bless this gift from God." Vitale shook his head and winced at his friend's words. "Out of it may come more than you imagine. Have you prayed? If you like, I will pray with you for healing."

"St. Venantius is bored with my prayers by now. I've serenaded him both in prose and verse, but he does nothing for me. He's only a local saint, after all, and maybe has no power outside his home town."

"Flippancy won't help you," Vitale said, leaning forward and putting his hand over his friend's. "Only faith. Look, we have an hour before dinner. Come with me to the church of Saints John and Paul. There's a statue there of St. Martin, the great holy man of Gaul. Many have touched it and been healed."

"What if I can't believe?" Fortunatus felt his heart beat faster and wondered if it knew better than his head what the saint might be able to do. "Would God heal me anyway?"

"If you're willing to believe, it is enough," Vitale said, rising and pulling up his friend with him. "You know of the great bishop and poet, St. Paulinus of Nola? How St. Martin touched his ruined eye and made him whole?"

"I know of his poetry, which I think suffered from his conversion. St. Martin healed his eye, but hurt his art."

"Martin turned Paulinus inward. Public life for this healed soul was no longer Roman administration, but service to Christ. So may it be with you." Vitale had a way of ending disputes with an appeal to religious authority, and the poet knew better than to argue with him.

The two men had often debated the stampede of the church away from contemplation of the merciful Christ toward the fear of God's judgment. Gold that had once enriched the emperor and nobility now poured into the hands of bishops. They not only took care of the public welfare but promised to remit sins, holding off the wrath of God. If Fortunatus's blindness was caused by his sin with Phoebe, Vitale reasoned, the poet must give all he had to God. Otherwise he would be doomed to hellfire. Fortunatus had given his gold to Phoebe, so he had nothing left to give God except himself. Vitale's logic was merciless, and Fortunatus felt too broken and weak to fight it.

Yet miracles had happened, he knew, when a saint took an interest in a sinner and interceded for him. The Christian literature of the past few hundred years was rich with examples of being healed by touching a saint's relic or by promising to become a monk. He would have to offer the saint some sort of vow, Fortunatus thought, to prove that he was ready to change. *Become a monk? Please, not that*, the poet prayed to St. Martin, conjuring up an image in his mind of the soldier-saint of Gaul. *But I will at least promise to sin no more with Phoebe. You saw how I sent her away? There, you have a vow of sorts.* He hoped that St. Martin, having been a soldier, would take the sin with Phoebe more lightly than his mother had.

Led by his friend, Fortunatus sensed the uneven pavement under his feet as he walked toward the low, domed church that had been built soon after the time of Constantine. *The streets might have lost their smooth Roman surface, and grass between the stones might tickle my toes, but the Church of Saints John and Paul*, Fortunatus thought, *have a floor perfect as that of paradise.* The times demanded new loyalties, after all, and like St. Paulinus, who had turned from governing to preaching, Fortunatus knew the future lay with Christianity.

I will write poems about saints if you heal me, Fortunatus vowed silently to St. Martin. Fearing that St. Martin might feel he was being bribed, Fortunatus began praying directly to the Lord Christ and felt a warmth in his heart that gave him hope his prayer was heard. *Despite my defects, God willing, I could perhaps be healed.* By the time they reached the church, Fortunatus was dizzy from breathing so fast and deeply. *I feel holy contrition*, he told himself, *I'm sorry for what I did with Phoebe, Lord, truly I am.*

The church was cold, as were the stones under Fortunatus's feet. He could feel the coolness through his thin sandals, as he felt the warmth of his friend's hand on his own. Since his blindness had overcome him after the sin with Phoebe, and even more after she left, Fortunatus had noticed that his other senses had become more acute. Even the distant scent of jasmine, which reminded him of Phoebe's perfume, was enough to make him weep. He could hear the echoes of their footsteps, rhythmic as drumbeats, and imagined himself part of a march of pilgrims, headed toward the throne of Christ, their feet pounding like the headache that was starting behind his eyes.

"Over here," Vitale said, pulling him sharply to the right. "Reach out and touch the statue of St. Martin. Hold still. I'll guide your hand. Ask and you shall receive. In his body's relics the saint still lives, growing hair and nails. There's magic in this place."

"I feel it," Fortunatus said, the words not coming with their usual ease. "Is it a healing magic? Or is it a miracle of God?" For a moment he felt the way he had when as a child he first received communion. His Lord was with him, in him, and he asked no questions, just tasted God.

"Magic or miracle, it's all mystery," Vitale whispered, reaching out to the lamp burning in front of the statue. "We are children in the lap of God. We need know no more than that."

Dipping one finger in the oil pooling at the base of the lamp, Vitale gently touched his friend's eyelids with it. Then he held up the right hand of the poet and laid it on St. Martin's cheek. Vitale's touch was warm, and the poet was suddenly struck by the love he felt for this friend of his childhood and the love Vitale had for him. *The communion of saints*, he said to himself, *it is love, and we share it even if we are far from saints ourselves.*

Still, in the back of his mind, he wondered if his contrition was real or just a performance, like declaiming to an audience an especially heartfelt poem. Realizing that he had grown so used to performing that he could no longer distinguish between genuine and theatrical emotion, Fortunatus stopped trying to pray. A silence came over his soul, as he felt the smooth stone of a face under his fingers, and touched the hollows that were the saint's eyes, the point of the aristocratic nose. His hand felt warmer, but his headache was worse, seeming to roar in waves against the back of his eyeballs. It reminded him of the waves of pressure and release he had felt when making love to Phoebe, but no child would be birthed from this fierce pain, this sense of sin washed away by an ocean of forgiving grace.

"O my God," he groaned, his hand sliding down to grasp St. Martin's stone shoulder. "Let your holy saint rescue me from blindness as he did Paulinus, and I will be your man." The promise frightened him, and he added, "In my own way." *Probably I've just spoiled the effect of my momentary belief and my friend's prayer, but that's my weakness, to take one step forward and two steps back.*

"Look, the statue is shining," Vitale said, his voice choking on the words. "St. Martin has heard you."

The setting sun poured in the small window near them and struck the marble, brightening the half-smile of the stone saint.

"I see it," Fortunatus said, and he did see it. The headache reached a piercing peak, finally exploding into silence and relief. "My sight is clear, praise God."

"Then you are now God's man, as you promised." Vitale released his friend's hand. "You must leave your Roman ways behind, Fortunatus, and find a new kind of life. You had thought merely to travel north, but now I think you will be making an inward journey, as well."

"I must do both," Fortunatus said, smiling in wonder as he looked around at the dim church, glowing in spaces favored by sunlight. "I must leave Ravenna and thank St. Martin at his shrine in Gaul. For me, Ravenna is over, and so is Italy. The emperor has seen to that for me, as he has for you."

"We will travel together from Padua on," Vitale said. "First, I must meet with the bishops of northern Italy."

Fortunatus felt his throat go dry. "What happens if the emperor's men catch you? Shouldn't you come with me now?" The road would be a lonely one without Vitale.

"You can go on by yourself as far as Padua. We can meet there and go north together. The Frankish rulers will shelter us, loving as they do all things Roman. But they understand *Romanitas* only a little, as a blind man understands light. You'll be St. Martin's poet and Christ's ambassador. What do you say to that?"

Fortunatus nodded, unable to speak. He had a moment's regret for the music, art, and city life he would be leaving behind, but he had promised. No turning back was possible. Boëthius had told his father that spirit was gone from the arts and from all the places that had given joy to his childhood. Only a dead shell was left, still and inhuman as the mosaic faces of the dead emperor and his dead wife.

These Frankish rulers who were friends of Vitale's might have need of a poet to sing their warlike songs, but in a softer voice than that of their savage bards. He might be able to lead them through his poetry into fields of flowers rather than fields of blood. They might even pay him for his efforts, if he praised them as he had not praised Justinian and Theodora. Fortunatus felt gleaming, polished words pulse in his ears and tingle in his fingertips. They would speak of a new order, sing a new song. He had promised, and God would bless him for it. Fortunatus knew a good bargain when he saw one. Leaving a ruined, soulless Italy behind suddenly did not seem so hard.

By the time Fortunatus set out for Francia, Justinian's conquest of Italy had brought more horror and chaos than it had imperial order. The plague had stripped the countryside of farmers and cities of their artisans and merchants. Whole towns lay empty, except for skeletons from the plague years. In some places no one remained alive to bury the dead. Too little of the old provincial nobility survived, retired in country estates, dreaming of the glorious past; too much of the new society was based on bureaucracy and bishops. Here and there something of Rome remained—in Ravenna where Justinian had built his western outpost and in Visigothic Spain, birthplace of Princess Brunhild, soon to be Queen of the Franks.

Fortunatus had heard of her. Who had not? She was beautiful, civilized, and destined to rule. Too bad, he thought, that she was an Arian. These great ladies, he said to Vitale, were either, like Theodora, obsessed with the belief that Christ was all God, or like Brunhild, that he was all man. *Pythagoras, and Boëthius after him, would have said the Christ was both, as are we all,* Fortunatus thought, *but extremes are the way of the world.* To take the middle road meant that one was not sufficiently enthused and thus was suspect in the eyes of true believers. He might be the last man in either the eastern or the western empire to carry the wisdom of Pythagoras and Boëthius, a wisdom comprised neither of clouds nor earth exclusively, but of a rainbow bridging the gap between the two.

Since earthly politics and romance had ruined him, Fortunatus felt he would do better to stick with clouds and art. He could have been on his way to Greece with Phoebe and their children, but instead was headed into the cold mists of the north, where no one knew him, classical poetry, or anything else worth knowing. Love of Phoebe had brought blindness on him, but gratitude to St. Martin had made him put away his childish passions. This time, he knew better than to rant with adolescent fury against great powers. He would instead praise them for their virtues and turn his face silently from their vices.

Reflecting on his offense against the great Emperor Justinian, Fortunatus had to admit that his epic poem on the emperor's invasion of Italy had been only a fine exhibit of vanity. In it, the youthful poet had called Theodora, Justinian's beloved wife, a harlot who had disgraced the throne and driven her husband into madness. These sins were common knowledge, but it was unwise to speak of them. Given the nature of his own sin, the poet knew he was hardly the man to point out an empress's scandalous past. It was no wonder that Theodora's nephew hated him and wanted him dead.

His course was northward, away from Rome, the poet knew, but he had to take one last look at the mosaics of the church where Justinian, the enemy, had left his image. The emperor had only recently died, but his power still hovered over Italy like a dark cloud, and his servant, General Narses, had made sure Fortunatus and the emperor's other enemies knew they were on borrowed time.

The poet stood with his travelling bag over his shoulder, and at his waist a flask of wine, that same flask that Rusticiana had filled from the cup of Boëthius. She had given it to Fortunatus's father, along with her husband's manuscripts. The flask dangled from the handle of his father's short sword. Down the block, Fortunatus could see the church of San Vitale glowing like a jewel in sunshine, a relic of the Rome he was about to leave. Slowly, wanting to prolong the moment, Fortunatus approached the carved doors, took off his sandals and entered the church. He looked up at the faces of Justinian and Theodora, who had left their mark in the form of mosaics, from which they looked down on worshippers like deities. Their severe, imperial faces were broken into a thousand pieces of shining stone.

In their images, Fortunatus saw the fractured power of the Roman world, broken but mysteriously one. *Maybe*, he thought, though reluctant to see any virtue in the imperial pair, *their vision is not dead, only sea-changed into an unrecognizable form, like a sword left underwater for a lifetime and turned a mottled green.* Where he was going, only change was certain. Nothing he saw would be familiar. All would be harsh and ragged with the barbarian edge that had cut its way into the Rome where his ancestors had been at home. Fortunatus left the great hall with its mosaics and speckled colors, knowing he would not see such profligate beauty again. It was just as well, he told himself. *The barbarians, not the meek, have inherited the earth, and I must cast my lot with these simple brutes. As I go, so goes the greatness that was once Rome, more's the pity. But maybe, more's the glory. Who knows what the barbarian kings of the north might give the world, if they are taught Romanitas?*

In this ambivalent state, the poet took his leave of the splendor and decadence of classical Rome. To his shame, the loss uppermost in his mind was that of fine wine and properly smoked oysters. In the future, he would no doubt have to live on beer, roots, and the half-cooked haunches of deer. He knew that the cold, wet north could not easily grow much more than oats and barley. Wheat was not an option. *Forget about grapes and olives,* Fortunatus warned himself. *I've heard that central Francia has a little grape culture, though its wine is no doubt as bad as its bread. But as long as its effect is the same as that of good Italian wine, I won't complain.*

After taking a swig from his flask, Fortunatus poured out a few drops of wine before a roadside shrine to Saints Peter and Paul. If the saints were thirsty, they would not be satisfied, but at least he had made a pious gesture. For good measure, he chanted a spell taught to him by his pagan nurse when he was a child, blowing all enemy spells away and casting ashes in the mouths of those who wished him ill. Feeling cleansed, cured, and in charge of his life, the poet started on his way.

Except for birdsong and the creaking and clunking of wooden logs in waterwheels, his solitude was uninterrupted by any sound. At first, he felt uneasy, not wanting to be thrown back on his small self for entertainment. All his life he had needed the presence of others and their admiration in order to feel satisfied. Phoebe had told him that he was like a dinner guest who could not simply enjoy the meal but had to talk to the host about what went into every dish. She had been right, the poet thought, for he could not even write his verses without wine, audience, and expectation of a patron's approval.

Inside, he felt hollow, as if a winter wind blew through him and rattled his bones. Then he began to listen only to the slush, slush of his leather boots on the wet, worn stones of the old Roman road, and thought of nothing at all. A peace fell over him, gentle as the coming of night, and he could wish himself in no other place or company. He wanted that peace to last forever, but knew his obsessive plans for the future and regrets for the past would not allow it.

Fortunatus broke his journey at the hilltop home of Rusticiana, to touch heart and forehead with the aged wife of Boëthius. The two sat on a marble bench in the overgrown gardens that had once belonged to Boëthius, but now, since the death of Theodoric, belonged to no one in particular. Few of the old, far-flung provincial estates remained occupied, unless by military commanders or bishops. It was easier for Rusticiana to be a squatter in her old home than to pay taxes to Rome as an owner. She was too broken in age and spirit to fight for what should have been hers. Fortunatus ceremoniously uncapped his flask and offered the old woman the last of his wine.

"Your husband once drank from this very flask, my father told me," Fortunatus said, looking sadly into its depths, wishing the vessel were not almost empty. "I like to think of this wine as the drink of heroes, on whose shoulders we ride like children."

"And like children, we don't know what the old ones knew," Rusticiana said, holding her wrinkled hands tightly together in her lap. "We never will, I'm afraid."

"Only God can see to the end of the long threads we've knotted with our little lives. The future is not ours to know, as the Lord Jesus himself said." Fortunatus thought he must remember these words for some later poem and longed to write them down.

"Or for us to have a stake in," said Rusticiana, refusing to be comforted. "I feel as if I am, as are we all, nothing more than dust motes whirling in patterns learned from the stars. I suppose I'm saying my husband died for nothing."

"We and the ones coming after us will make something new." Fortunatus set the stopper in his empty flask. "I must believe that or despair. That's why I'm going north to live with the barbarian Franks. The future lies there, not with the poor, dying villages of Italy. I've seen them, and they make me sick. Let the dead bury their dead."

Rusticiana wiped the red drops off her lips with the sleeve of her ragged gown. "I wasn't allowed to bury my dead. Instead, I stay in my husband's house and tend his hearth-fire. But you must have the ring of Pythagoras, my young friend. Boëthius wanted you to wear it and carry on his work."

The ring glowed in the light of the afternoon sun that shone through the tall cypress trees ringing the estate. Fortunatus caught his breath as the old woman slipped the ring from her finger and handed it to him.

"Great ones wore it in the past," she said. "May it be a blessing on your journey to a new life."

Letters that Fortunatus could not read were carved on the inside surface. "Can you read the inscription?"

Rusticiana shook her head, and tendrils of lank white hair came loose from her braid. "I don't recognize the language. Not Greek, certainly. My husband saw something like this lettering carved on a barbarian sword, but even he could make nothing of it."

Fortunatus put the ring on his finger, wishing he could know the message it carried. Still, he felt a thrill of power and strength touch him like the lightning of love, as the gold warmed his skin. *It is not*, he felt, *a gift for me, but for an unknown someone who in the future will bring light to the world.* He was only its guardian, as he was the guardian of much else, if he could manage to save any of his culture from oblivion. He would be lucky to save himself, Fortunatus thought, coming back to common earth. Even now, the soldiers of General Narses were likely to be pursing him. He needed a talisman that would bring him good luck, but doubted that even the ring of Pythagoras would get him safely beyond the emperor's reach.

As he left Rusticiana's hilltop hiding-place, the poet wondered if the ring might be cursed. He thought of Boëthius's fate at the hands of King Theodoric. Would he himself fare any better among the Frankish kings? It crossed his mind that neither spirit nor wisdom would be valued in the age he saw coming, but he banished the premonition with a song. His voice was so rich and sweet that the birds joined in and kept him company as he walked northward.

Fortunatus met Vitale just beyond Padua, after crossing the River Po. It had been a hard journey thus far, he explained to his friend over dinner in a priest's home on the outskirts of the city. The roof was thatched with reeds, and the windows were shuttered with willow weavings covered with clay and cow dung, creating a smell that turned Fortunatus's stomach. Inside, the floor was littered with rushes in which blowfly maggots germinated amid chicken bones and other refuse meant for the dogs that nosed and ate the human leavings. The autumn wind swept down off the western Alps and blew in through the ill-fitting door. Both men shivered until the priest's wife brought each of them a sheepskin wrap. Fortunatus warmed himself with wine, while Vitale drank his usual plain water, sipping thoughtfully as he stared into the fire on the stone hearth.

"After I crossed the Po," Fortunatus said, wiping his full lips carefully with his tongue, so as not to waste any of the wine, however sour it was, "I felt I had fallen off the cliff of civilization. My Latin is barely understood, so much has the speech of the Goths corrupted our own, at least among the common people."

"But not, I think, among the clergy and the landowners," Vitale replied. "The barbarians flow in like the tide, and their brackish water mingles with the pure rivers of our mountains. In time, they'll be gentled by religion and the old culture. Already the Franks of the north are being turned Roman. You'll see."

"Theodoric and his Goths were bad enough. Now the Lombards, hairy lips and all, plan to come from the north and wreck whatever the others left behind. I take your word for it that the Franks have something better to offer."

Vitale smiled. "I believe King Sigibert does, though his brothers are like wild boars. Sigibert is a great warrior in the old tradition, but a modest man, learned in the classics and a virtuous Catholic. His marriage to Brunhild, the princess from Spain, will bring about a new Rome in the north, or so all our clergy hopes. Our own journey to Metz should converge with Brunhild's entourage this coming spring, if God wills."

"I'm already composing the wedding poem that will bring me to the royal couple's notice," Fortunatus told his friend. "If they're as cultivated as you say, I may make a place for myself at court. Nothing else would suit me in the barbarian north, certainly not the Church as a career. If the king and his new queen hope to create a new Rome, they'll need another Virgil, or what, in these wretched times, passes for one."

"My friend Praetextatus is bishop of Rouen. He'll give you the introduction you need. We'll stop with him before going to the royal wedding in Metz. Show him this marriage poem of yours, and ask him to help you win these royal patrons. Without them, you have no hope of a life at court. If anyone is to make the new Rome rise from the ashes of the old, it's King Sigibert of Austrasia. People with any sense wish he were king of all Francia."

They both fell silent, looking into the flames. Fortunatus remembered the dream of Theodoric, called the Great, to restore the grandeur that was Rome. The barbarian king had been a hostage in Constantinople and educated for ten formative years in the old Roman style. Still, he had gone back to his people's savage ways and died a violent death. Who could tell if Sigibert wouldn't do the same, despite the civilizing influence of Princess Brunhild?

Fortunatus shook his head, which was hurting with wine and regret. He wished that his historical memory were not so keen. Unlike the stable, serene Greek empire, the Latin world seemed doomed to factional fighting. It was led by a church militant, not a church of scholars and mystics. Feeling a sudden chill, he threw another log on the fire. Perhaps he too would meet the fate of Boëthius in his attempt to bring Roman graces to the wild boars of the north.

A pounding on the door shook the house, and woke up the priest. Fearing attack, Fortunatus pulled out his sword and followed the priest across the room. Vitale staggered out from under his sheepskin, sleepy, but available for battle, if he were needed. When the priest called out to the intruders, asking what they wanted, there was a brief silence.

"We come peacefully," one rough voice answered. "Our master, General Narses, has sent us to arrest the poet Fortunatus, who insulted the Empress Theodora. In the name of the Greek Imperium, admit us."

The priest turned to Fortunatus, spreading his hands in confusion. "Who shall I say you are?" he whispered. "We have no choice but to let the emperor's men in."

Fortunatus felt his cheeks redden, and his hands shook so much that he dropped the sword with a clank on the stone floor. He thought fast and glanced at Vitale. "Maybe representatives of the church, on our way to the Frankish king's wedding?"

"We are Sidonius and his servant, sent by the bishop of Ravenna," Vitale said, nodding at his host. "Tell them that."

The frightened priest admitted the three men, who came in stamping the snow off their leather boots and cursing the sudden blizzard. They pulled out their swords, stood back to back in a triangle, and glared at the priest's other visitors. The priest hastened to tell them what Vitale had said, and beckoned to his wife to bring beer and bread for the soldiers. The leader of the three stared first at Vitale and then at Fortunatus, who had picked up his sword and was trying to appear as if he knew how to use it.

"You look like no poet I've ever seen," said the leader. "Maybe you are who you say you are. You're too tall and thick in the shoulders to be a scribbler."

Fortunatus smiled and put his sword back in its sheath."Right," he said. "I can't even print my name, let alone compose a poem. Here, man, have something to warm you. This cold's enough to freeze a man's guts."

Fortunatus sat with the soldiers while they ate. He told them stories and poured them more beer until finally they puked and slid to the floor in a besotted heap. Over their stinking, sprawled bodies, his eyes met Vitale's. Without speaking, they agreed to move on. The priest and his wife supplied them with food for their journey and hurried them off, clearly hoping their two guests would not be caught by Narses' soldiers, then questioned in unpleasant and irresistible ways. Hospitality to the eastern emperor's enemies would be frowned upon, and the priest knew it. Better to send his dangerous visitors packing.

As Fortunatus and Vitale travelled over what was left of the Via Claudia Augusta to Aquileia, then through the Carnic Alps, they often looked behind them, wondering if they were being followed. The pair zigzagged off and onto the road along the Lech, crossing the river wherever they could, then crossing back, hoping to avoid any pursuers. They passed fields where iron-bladed ploughs were dragged by oxen, one farmer walking behind the plough and the other at the side of the ox. So farmers had walked in the ancient Roman era, but no one could be sure that fields would go on being tilled for much longer. Few farmers were left since the plague had struck a generation before. In time of war and heavy taxation, many of the remaining farmers ran away from their land, hiding in the hills. *Maybe they had the right idea*, the poet thought, and wondered if he, too, should hide from both invaders and tax-collectors, not to mention Emperor Justin's pursuing soldiers.

While he walked, Fortunatus composed a long poem in his head, recounting the cruel history of the Franks he was going to meet in Metz. Even the name of Clovis, or Chlodovech, meant "pillaging warrior," he remembered Vitale saying, not exactly an encouraging start to the new order in Gaul. When he was just fifteen years of age, Clovis had started his reign with only Belgium as an inheritance. By the time he was thirty, he ruled over all the Franks. The word 'Frank' came from *Frekkr*, the "fierce ones," and Clovis lived up to the name. The king destroyed so many of his competing kin that when it came time for him to die, he mourned that he had no more relatives to comfort him. *Of course not*, Fortunatus thought, *since you killed them all*. Instead of joining the Goths in Arianism, Clovis followed the faith of his Burgundian Queen. By becoming a Catholic, he linked his Franks with the Romans in one church, a stroke that brought him an empire.

Clovis meant to found an imperial dynasty. His son Chlothar, however, was not the equal of his father. No dreams of Rome for him, only lust for treasure and women. Vitale had told Fortunatus that Chlothar's four battling sons, except for Sigibert, were no better, wallowing in concubines and bloody civil wars. Fortunatus wondered if Sigibert would be able to overcome the bad blood of his family, and not for the first time, asked himself also if he were walking into a prison worse than the one that had swallowed Boëthius in Pavia. He turned the ancient ring on his finger and tried to think of Pythagoras, whose luminous vision had brightened the last days of Boëthius. For a moment, he felt the touch of God, as he had when St. Martin cured his eyes, and he found himself praying for the theological virtue of hope as he left the snow-capped Alps behind him.

The priest's house near the Italian Alps had been a palace, Fortunatus grumbled to his friend, compared to the rough hill-town of Aguntum, with its century old *castella*, built in a last-ditch effort to hold back the flood of barbarians from Germany. And the bishop's home in Aguntum had, in turn, been a mansion compared to Augsberg on the Lech River. Heavy dark clouds and bouncing hail drove the pilgrims into the shrine of St. Afra, where they gratefully prayed, ate, and slept on benches lining the back of the small, low-ceilinged church. Fortunatus stared into the roundness of the dome, dimly lit with malodorous candles made from animal fat, and considered his situation. He had hoped to find the beginnings of a new Roman empire, one that would offer a cultured man like himself a home and a living. Instead, he was coming to think that no one here in the north much cared about Roman culture or about an empire that would span all of Francia, offering peace and progress. *Survival is what they care about, and perhaps,* Fortunatus thought, *I should follow their example.*

He had a serious hangover and trouble holding down the beans and bacon given to the pilgrims by the bishop of Innsbruck. As he walked, he sang his poems to the ice-broken pine trees along what was left of the Roman road skirting the old frontier. Whenever the two friends stopped at rundown estates where a rural priest or bishop maintained a precarious residence, Fortunatus declaimed his poems to anyone who would listen. He was unsure whether or not his hearers understood his rhetorical flourishes, but at least they paid attention and a little money, too. At their last stop, Fortunatus learned that Narses' men had continued to pursue them. The soldiers had heard that the same sturdy swordsman they had drunk with in Italy had been reciting classical verse to his hosts along the Danube. *Curse my vanity,* Fortunatus thought, wiping away the snow from his mustache and beard. He had hoped to pass for a barbarian, but the sparse hair on his face was unlikely to fool anyone.

A few miles from Metz, the poet and his friend stopped again to rest, then moved on when they heard that the royal procession was approaching the city. It would be easier to evade their pursuers, Vitale decided, once they had joined the crowded wedding festivities. Fortunatus insisted on stopping for dinner at a villa still run by a Roman caretaker, standing in for his absentee senatorial owner. The fellow was happy to take a few coins from the pilgrims in return for a room and food.

Fortunatus knew that to earn recognition and sanctuary from the king and his bride, he would need to finish his wedding poem. King Sigibert would certainly turn him over to the eastern emperor's men unless the poet had first been able to win his favor. All night, while Vitale slept by the fire, the poet drank and wrote, his verses growing more extravagant in their praise of the wedding couple as his cup emptied.

Brunhild, he wrote, was a princess glowing with the light of imperial grace, and Sigibert a paragon of princely glory. Luckily he had learned from the local priest that Brunhild had recently turned Catholic. Now he could write that the royal pair shared religion as well as a throne. Together they would rebuild ancient Rome in a new land he wrote. They would be rising suns like rulers of the past, warriors carrying the banner of salvation. 'Sig' was the Germanic name for sun and for victory, so the poet was not stretching his metaphor too far. He knew his sources were pagan and would be frowned on by conservative churchmen, but also knew that Sigibert was a man barely out of a pagan world.

Fortunatus drew courage from the new buildings, frescoes, and mosaics he saw around him, signs that the Merovingian dynasty took seriously its ties to imperial Rome. With this happy inspiration, he created his poetic vision of a Roman, Christian, yet vigorously Frankish empire. By morning, he was exhausted and out of wine, but the wedding poem lay complete before him on the rough wooden table. If it did not dazzle the hearts of the royal couple and make them proud to be rulers of the New Rome, he was no judge of human nature. Overcome by drink and sleep, Fortunatus let his face fall on his manuscript and dreamed of improbable palaces in the snow-wrapped north.

As they ate breakfast the next morning, Vitale told his friend all he could remember of Merovingian plots and counterplots, hoping Fortunatus could pick his way among the hostilities of kings, clerics, and *comitates*, or warrior nobles. All four kings were sons of Chlothar and kept an uneasy truce with each other. The kings hungered for the civilized image that *Romanitas* would give them; the *comitates* hungered for independence from a central government; the clerics, mostly Gallo-Romans and Romanized Franks, hungered to regain the power of their long-ago senatorial predecessors. Each of the competing groups was busy creating new buildings and adorning them.

Since the builders could rely only on local craftsmen, the art was necessarily simple and stiff in execution. Still, the friezes and frescoes had a fine military strength and brilliant color to recommend them. By echoing these artistic efforts, the poet hoped he could win the favor of kings and nobles.

His poetry would be shaped by the new style and would stimulate, in turn, the arts that could make outposts like Metz and Soissons into miniature Romes. Vitale did not need to tell him any more. Fortunatus saw his course, and if he were given the chance to stand before the king and queen, he knew exactly what he wanted to say. When Vitale took him to visit Bishop Praetextatus on a spring morning in 566, Fortunatus was relieved to learn that the bishop, despite his timid conventionality, could appreciate the poet's verses and would approve their presentation to the royal couple.

The cathedral of Metz was impressive, though unfinished. Like other northern churches, even cathedrals, it was made of timbers rather than stone. *They won't last like the churches of Italy*, thought Fortunatus, *for these Frankish buildings can too easily be burned down by barbarian marauders.* Some rough attempts at full-sized statuary made the poet wince, when he remembered the great basilica in Ravenna. He hoped the cultivated princess from southern Spain would not be repelled by the clumsy efforts of the northern builders. *At least she'll enjoy the refinement of my poetry*, Fortunatus told himself. *And she'll know that not all men in Francia are without culture.*

Several rows of noblemen stood awaiting the royal couple, lining the cobblestone road leading up to the church. *They don't look especially noble,* Fortunatus thought. Some could pass as farmers or tradesmen, but for their fine swords. Vitale had explained to him that the *comitates* were not of the senatorial class, as in old Rome, but a motley mix of men who had probably stolen the money to buy a sword and a horse. They might have come from peasant families or be sons of warriors, but they all clustered around a king or duke, hoping for preferment and loot, utterly dependent on their warlord's strength and generosity.

They raised their swords in the air as Sigibert approached in a horse-drawn cart decorated with banners and flowers. Fortunatus was glad of his height, which allowed him to see over the heads of others in the crowd. He saw a man even taller than he was, decked in a plumed Roman helmet that shone brassily in the noon sun. Sigibert held the reins of the four horses himself, seeming oblivious to the failure of his cart to equal the elegance of a Roman chariot. The young king had a firm jaw, blond hair spreading over his shoulders and down his back, and a wide, full-lipped smile that was marred only by a missing side tooth. He raised one hand in salute to his waiting *comitates*, then looked back at the cart that followed his.

Fortunatus and the crowd stared too, as the famous Princess Brunhild came into view. She, too, held the reins herself, and looked to be as tall as her man. Her face was round and childlike, her sparkling blue-green eyes were wide-spaced, and her skin smooth and white as cream. Thick, light brown hair spread around her like wings in the wind. Fortunatus caught his breath at the sight, wishing he could recompose her description in his poem, doing justice to it. The princess was full-figured and regal, no mere slip of a girl. She carried power in her and the crowd knew it. Everyone bowed as she went by, and murmured her name like a prayer. When his cart reached the church door, Sigibert tossed the reins to one of his men, jumped down, and hurried to Brunhild. She reached out to him, and he swung her into the air and down beside him, holding her close. The two gazed into each others' eyes, and then pulled slowly apart. Hand in hand, they walked toward the church.

Nobles and guests followed at a respectful distance. Fortunatus and Vitale stayed close behind Bishop Praetextatus, who had promised to introduce the poet to the royal pair at dinner, after the ceremony. Spring flowers had been scattered on the church floor, while the small windows had been covered with bright-colored banners that cast vari-colored light across the church when the sun shone through the cloth. The altar toward which

Sigibert and Brunhild walked, still holding hands, was decked with glossy silk that fluttered in the gusts from the open wooden doors.

Fortunatus edged as close to Bishop Praetextatus as he could get, finally standing right behind the carved, high-backed chair in which the bishop was seated. From there, he was able to see the couple in profile, whenever they were not turning their heads to look into each others' eyes. Hearing the words of the wedding ceremony, Fortunatus was overcome with pique that he had not thought to include them in his poem, which seemed overly ornate and pagan compared to the words of the liturgy said by the Bishop of Metz.

The marriage of the two rulers was like the union of Christ and his church, the bishop chanted. The man and woman would become one flesh, their love binding them to each other and their people in harmony. Looking down at his feet, clad in thong-wrapped leather boots, Fortunatus felt embarrassed that his own poem fell so far short of the words and images in the wedding liturgy. Simplicity, he thought, was a virtue he had never cultivated, or even valued, until now. Still, the wedding poem, as Bishop Praetextatus had so kindly said, would remind hearers that imperial majesty still reigned in Francia as it had in the days of Caesar Augustus.

Fortunatus glanced around him at the nobles, clothed in trousers, hip-length woolen tunics, and furs, then at the altar's roughly shaped gold accoutrements lit by lumpish candles spitting animal fat as they burned. *Not much imperial majesty to be found here,* the poet thought, and sighed to think of his oratorical pearls soon to be cast before swine. Wild boars of the north, Rusticiana had called them, rooting for their dinners at the trough of the barbarian kings. *Since I myself hope to join them at the same trough,* Fortunatus thought, *I should not be so quick to judgment.*

Vitale pointed out Chilperic, king of western Francia, a ferret-faced man with none of his brother's muscled bulk. Next to Chilperic were his two grown sons, one of whom stared at Brunhild as if she were the burning bush.

The young fellow was tall, thin, and scholarly, looking far more like a poet than Fortunatus himself did. Behind Chilperic stood his concubine Fredegund, her waist-long, pale blond hair unbound like a virgin's, her large brown eyes innocent as a child's. As everyone had told him, Fortunatus thought, staring at the harlot, she was startlingly beautiful, enough to set a man's heart pounding as he wondered what that full body would look like unwrapped from its silks and furs. As he stared, her eyes met his and Fredegund smiled, her pointy, catlike little teeth framed by her plump red lips.

Ever politic, Fortunatus bowed his head slightly, acknowledging her notice, but in his veins a chill spread. The small, sumptuous woman laughed knowingly and tossed her head, so that the waves of pale hair shook like gold silk. Chilperic glanced back at her, and she was suddenly all his, her eyes half-closed, her lips pouting in a blown kiss. *Such a woman should not have been brought to the wedding of a princess as pure as Brunhild,* he thought, and wondered if Sigibert felt the same way he did. The prince looked resolutely away from the other royal pair, but smiled at his brother Guntram of Burgundy, a burly fellow who stood at Sigibert's side in support and fealty. The two men were friends as well as brothers, Vitale had told him, and they considered their kingdoms to be as one. Since Guntram had no living children, Sigibert would be his heir.

"And over there," Vitale said, nudging him and surreptitiously pointing at a tall, slender woman draped from head to toe in soft, gray and white wool, as were the three women accompanying her, "is Queen Radegund, founder of the monastery of the Holy Cross in Poitiers. A saint, people call her."

For a moment Fortunatus thought he was going blind again, so radiant was the face of this queen turned nun, this woman who seemed to have precipitated out of his imagination and into the world men assumed was real. She did not look at him, but only at the royal couple, her lips moving in prayer, her silvery, shining eyes looking at them or perhaps through them, seeing more than Fortunatus and the others could. Radegund's long, delicate nose seemed to breathe something sweeter than the common air. Her high-boned, glowing cheeks reminded Fortunatus of the faces of children he had seen in the mountains, blazoned by sun and wind. The queen had to be at least forty, he knew, but she had the ageless look of a statue copied from Praxiteles's Venus, a perfect incarnation of spirit in flesh, Pythagoras would have said, a seamless union of the divine and the human.

O God, behold one like your virgin mother, Fortunatus thought, then glanced around him, fearful that he had spoken the words aloud. *I'm unworthy even to see her face or breathe the air she breathes. Strike me dead if I ever think an evil thought of her.*

He had to grasp the tall back of Bishop Praetextatus's chair to steady himself. *This woman is beyond me, and I must not look at her anymore,* the poet thought, trembling in his depths, *or I will fall, a servant, at her feet.* She was something more than human, like the mosaic icons of saints he had seen in Ravenna, and she would break him like an unruly horse if he let her near him. Fortunatus had things to do before surrendering himself to anyone and was determined to stay away from a woman who could disrupt his worldly destiny. Radegund could do that, he knew, so she must be avoided like lightning or fire. He was and would be his own man. And St. Martin's, he was careful to add, fearful that the saint would feel betrayed and take back the gift of sight.

When the ceremony was over, the dignitaries passed out of the church behind the royal couple. Praetextatus hurried his two Italian friends along with him to the royal palace, where the wedding banquet would take place and Fortunatus could afterwards deliver his wedding poem. As they walked the short street to the palace, Fortunatus turned to look behind him. What he saw made him draw in his breath sharply. The poet nudged Vitale to look, too.

"Narses' soldiers," Vitale whispered and went pale remembering the near-attack at Aguntum. "We must stay close to the bishop."

"If these men say they're representatives of Emperor Justin," Fortunatus whispered back, "they'll be admitted to the banquet along with us. And there they can make their move."

"Cutting us down in the emperor's name wouldn't get them punished. You must speak your poem to Sigibert first, so he will favor you with protection. I'll tell the bishop."

Vitale moved forward and laid his hand on the arm of Bishop Praetextatus and spoke to him. Fortunatus turned again and looked for their pursuers, but could not distinguish them from the crowd of *comitates* and church dignitaries following the royal procession. He scurried in the bishop's wake, ducking his head, trying to be invisible. Once in the rough-hewn, single story stone palace, rebuilt from some earlier Roman villa, Fortunatus felt safer. He stayed beside his friend, linking his arm in the crook of Vitale's. He stared around him at the irregular stone walls, stuffed with tiny pebbles where the rocks failed to fit each other, and at the high, timbered ceiling that came to a point over the center of the main hall. A hearth-fire burned under the peak of the roof, with stately, carved chairs before it, decked with pink and white flowers in honor of the newly wedded pair.

As soon as Brunhild and Sigibert were seated, Bishop Praetextatus stepped forward, asking permission for his friend, the poet Fortunatus, to deliver a wedding gift to them. Before they could answer, Narses's three soldiers leaped on Fortunatus and dragged him before the thrones. Fortunatus's heart was pounding, and for once, he could not say a word. His knees gave way beneath him and his stomach tossed, quaking with a fear so intense he thought he would vomit. *Not exactly the impression I hoped to make on the royal couple*, Fortunatus thought, part of him standing back and looking on the scene as on a play or a recitation. Instead of delivering a gorgeously latinate wedding poem, he would deliver the remains of his breakfast, and probably be hacked to death as well. *Vanity of vanities*, he thought, remembering the words of Ecclesiastes, *all is vanity. I will be a ridiculous figure as I die, and I deserve to be, for my presumption. God, I ask your forgiveness for my stupid sins. Receive me into your hands, and I will ask nothing more.*

"This man has defamed the great Empress Theodora," shouted the head of Narses' soldiers. "The emperor in Constantinople has decreed that he be killed for his offense. Do we have your permission, majesty?"

The king swept his hand in front of him, thumb down, not bothering to speak as he decreed the death sentence. Fortunatus tried to pray, but his mind seemed stuck like a cart wheel in mud. So ended the vanity of his foolish hopes for preferment and applause. Nothing could save him now, he felt, and nothing should. He touched the diamond in the ring of Pythagoras, hoping the relic would find a worthier home.

"Stop, in the name of our divine Savior," cried a woman's vibrant, deep voice, "The poet must not be harmed. King Sigibert, I ask you to free this innocent man as a favor to your step-mother and Francia's one-time queen."

Fortunatus dared to look up and saw that Queen Radegund had stepped out of the crowd and stood before the royal couple. She looked from them to him, and her shining, light gray eyes seemed to the poet as if they were windows into heaven. For such a glimpse of the divine, Fortunatus thought, he would gladly die at that very moment. But Sigibert nodded to Radegund and gave Fortunatus back his life, at least for the time being.

"Stand away from this man," the king said. "Let someone who knows him speak of his innocence or guilt."

Bishop Praetextatus gathered the folds of his heavy woolen cloak around him and stepped forward beside Radegund. "He is a poet from Italia who brings you and your queen a poem of your marriage that will make it live forever in the minds of men." The slight, bald bishop's voice shook. "Hear him, I beg you, and then decide if he should live or die."

"So be it," said King Sigibert, and glanced, smiling, at his queen. "You should hear your praises from some other mouth than mine, one better fitted to describe you, my Brunhild. So, poet, begin your poem. If it is good in our ears, it will save your life."

Fortunatus trembled as the soldiers of Narses let him go and walked back to their place in the crowd. The eyes of everyone were on him as he straightened his disordered clothes and took a few deep breaths to steady his voice. From the corner of his eye he could see Vitale, pale and frightened, clinging to Praetextatus's arm. Fortunatus rejoiced in the perfect memory that required no written text to prompt it. His small Greek harp sang under his fingers, and music surged within him. He chanted his verses as if he were a bishop chanting the wedding liturgy.

At first his voice was soft.

"In early spring when earth is freed of frost,
 And fields are dressed in grassy tapestries,
 Woods grow up the sides of mountain peaks,
 And green leaves are reborn on spreading trees. . ."

As he sang of grapes swelling on vines and bees perpetuating life and the joy of warmth returning to a cold, barren world, Fortunatus made his rich voice ring against the stone walls. He rolled on, commending the warriors who converged around their king like snowy slopes reaching to a mountain peak. Among these rough warlords, after all, he hoped to find patrons and a home. Fortunatus called Sigibert a sun king who lit the earth like a god. The reference might be too pagan to suit the clergy, but the poet noticed a smile on the king's face.

Sigibert sometimes looked puzzled and glanced up at the priest beside him for a translation, but on the whole, he seemed to grasp the grand Latin of Fortunatus's wedding song. He yawned only once, toward the last, but graciously inclined his head as the poet concluded with a reference to peace and heirs, subjects dear to his heart, from what Vitale had told Fortunatus. In the poet's soul, a blessing rose that made him think of Radegund, praying down God's love on the king and his bride. He hoped his words did justice to the rush of spirit that filled him at the end.

> *"Through your blessed rule may all our joys increase,*
> *May concord reign and all the world love peace.*
> *With children may you grant your people's prayer,*
> *And grandchildren to you may children bear."*

When he finished, he sank to his knees, suddenly weak, as the music left him. He looked up at Queen Brunhild, whose blue eyes crinkled at the corners as she smiled and then whispered in Sigibert's ear. Their heads stayed close together for a long moment, and at last Sigibert nodded.

"You have won your life, poet," the king said. "Your enemies will leave this place and tell their honored master that you are under my protection, forgiven for any crimes you may have committed in your youth."

He gestured to a man behind him, a small, graceful fellow dressed in a Roman toga that looked absurd in a place filled with barbarian warriors wearing their warm trousers. Even in Constantinople, no one wore the toga anymore, Fortunatus knew, wondering what strange devotion to the past possessed this man.

"Gogo, take our poet into your care and give him what he needs to follow our court."

Gogo, the small man, readjusted his toga self-consciously, and went to Fortunatus, taking the poet's arm. The two stepped to the side of Sigibert's throne, and Fortunatus knew he was safe. He watched Narses's soldiers leave the hall, took a breath so deep it was a prayer in itself, and smiled at Vitale across the room. He did not dare look at Radegund or thank her, for fear his calm would desert him, and, out of gratitude, he would faint or weep at her feet. His thanks would have to wait.

It was less than a year before Fortunatus saw Radegund again. She had summoned him through Gogo, their mutual friend, because a political crisis threatened to destroy the fragile peace among the Meroving brothers. As he rode his mule through the winter mud collecting on the once-smooth Roman road to Poitiers, Fortunatus mused over what the trouble might be. There were so many crises, Radegund could take her pick. Probably the one she was concerned about was the death of Charibert, the chinless, shifty king who was Chlothar's oldest, least attractive son. He had died of drink, not long after Fortunatus had seen him at the royal wedding in Metz. It was likely that no one mourned him except his mother, but his lands would be coveted by the other Merovings. *Enough to fight a war over them? Probably,* the poet thought. *These savages would fight like dogs over a bone, let alone a kingdom.*

Fortunatus looked around him at the late winter landscape, bleached here and there with snowdrifts, and graced with hardly any huts or hearth-fires. Even with the great migration of Franks from the north, the center of Francia was not populated as it once had been. When Radegund chose the region for her new monastery, she might have hoped it would be a desert lonely as St. Anthony's in Egypt. But it was only a semi-rural retreat connected by a passageway to the walls of Poitiers. The bishop of this town had offered her refuge and protection. Radegund had surely had enough experience in the world to know she would need both.

One of her greatest supporters, Fortunatus had heard from Vitale, was the tiny, sickly Gregory, a priest in Tours whose acquaintance the poet had been hoping to make. Gregory was from a Roman family that could claim a lineage as ancient as the empire itself. It was thought that if he lived, he would someday be a bishop, given his family connections, his charities, and his energy. Despite his physical frailty, Gregory was already a formidable figure in Francia and could only become more so as he came into his thirties.

Fortunatus could not help thinking that Gregory might be a potential patron who could well have more permanence and power than the evanescent Merovingian kings. They, after all, were likely to murder each other before they could fulfill promises to their followers. Radegund, with her royal and episcopal connections, might prove an even better patron, and Fortunatus meant to cultivate her as well. He was pledged to serve St. Martin, yes, but in his heart of hearts, the poet still served his own needs. *I live in this world, not the next. Soon enough the next will swallow me, but until then, I'll take good care of myself, as I always have.*

With his priorities firmly in place, Fortunatus knocked on the heavy gate of the abbey. Vitale had told him that Radegund had staffed her retreat with women who, like herself, had had enough of the world and its illusions. The queen had bought the land and restored the great house with the money King Chlothar had given her when she left him. People said it was to atone for his sins against his young bride that he paid her whatever she asked. The lecherous old king had never been known to care about his sins before, so it was a mystery, Vitale declared, why Chlothar had suddenly become so generous to this woman who had rejected him and the throne of Francia in order to serve God.

Fortunatus was surprised to see that the nun who opened the door was Radegund herself. He bowed to her on one knee and looked down at the neatly swept entry way that marked the liminal space between Poitiers and the sacred land of the abbey.

"Your majesty, I didn't think to see you as a servant in your own convent."

Radegund's laughter had a husky, intimate sound that made Fortunatus want to laugh, too. "Did Our Lord not call himself the servant of all? Are we better than our master?"

The abbey was oddly situated, extending from the city wall out into the countryside around Poitiers. It had been a Roman villa, and still had the cottages, barns, porticoes, and bathhouse that had made it comfortable in the last days of the empire. Gardens surrounded the small stone chapel near the villa, and Fortunatus appreciatively sniffed the air, fragrant with herbs and flowers. *A perfect place, a locus amoenus,* he thought, *where time seems to stand still.* For a moment he imagined himself back in Ravenna, before the ruin of the empire. He glanced up at the wall, noticing towers that stood high over the abbey, giving it the look of an armed camp, in contrast to the convent's pastoral interior. *Et in Arcadia ego,* he almost said aloud. *And here I am in an earthly paradise.* Unlike the tranquil Roman villas of the past, he thought, this one was a product of the violent and uncertain present. Security was only an illusion, even in this garden, this terrestrial heaven.

As he followed Radegund's gray clad figure through the courtyard, where chickens scratched and clucked, Fortunatus admired her form, straight and slender as a girl's.

"But you're a queen," he said, trying to understand. "Couldn't others tend the door and any guests?"

Radegund sat him down across from her at a rough, stained oak table. "I made a good woman, Leubovera, my abbess, and apart from being overfond of backgammon, she has done well at the job." The queen set a few dishes on the table. "We stand on no ceremony here. He who is first, is last, as the Gospel says."

Having no answer, the poet sat silent, staring into the silvery eyes that seemed to see through him. *No use making small talk with this one. She would think less of me for it.* He sipped the water she had given him, wishing it were something stronger. Still, the gentle warmth that spread through him at the sight of this woman worked as well as wine to quiet his restless mind.

"You may wonder why I have asked for you," Radegund said, arranging some nuts and mushrooms on the wooden plate before him. "We hardly know each other."

"I know that I owe you my life." Fortunatus tucked a few nuts into each mushroom cap before eating. He sighed, thinking that his beloved smoked oysters would have done nicely on top.

"Can I return the favor in some way? You have only to ask." He hoped she would ask nothing more strenuous than a poem in honor of some religious festival or other.

"Then I shall." Radegund leaned forward and her gray veil shadowed her face. "You know that King Charibert is dead, God rest his soul."

Fortunatus nodded, thinking she wanted him to write an elegy for the fallen king, and wondered what good he could say of the wretched man. He had spent some weeks at Charibert's court and had found the king's succession of wanton wives, if they could so be called, sickening enough to make him glad the monarch was untimely dead. Perhaps he could give Radegund a piece of the long encomium he had insincerely put together to honor Charibert while he had been entertained at the late king's court in Paris. Somehow he felt ashamed to recite it for this otherworldly nun, who surely knew the details of Charibert's graceless life.

"You've been at court long enough to know what happens when a king dies," Radegund went on, her long, white fingers twisting around the roughly-carved wooden cross hanging from her neck by a leather thong. "His brothers will fight each other for the lands left without a master. Even now, Chilperic is moving to take Tours and Poitiers, which Charibert wanted Sigibert to have. I would prefer not to have Chilperic as an overlord."

"How can that be avoided?" Fortunatus kept his eyes on her hands, not wanting to fall into the pale depths of her gray eyes, which drew him down to areas of his soul he preferred not to explore. *Let my sins remain a secret to her*, he thought, *for if she knew me well, she would think me no better than lechers like Charibert and Chilperic.*

"You have the gift of persuasive words," Radegund said, laying her hands on the table. "I would like you to prepare a letter to King Guntram and take it to his court in Burgundy. My hope is that he will throw his armies behind Sigibert's and force Chilperic to make peace. It would save many lives. Will you do this for me?"

At first Fortunatus considered her proposal in silence, running through its implications. *King Guntram would be yet another rich patron and Burgundy yet another court to applaud my poems. If I succeed, I will have the thanks of two monarchs, in addition to Radegund's. Though Chilperic might be a formidable enemy. I must be careful that he does not learn of this mission to Guntram. Chilperic and Fredegund would have my head, if they knew I was part of a conspiracy against their rule.*

Then he looked again into Radegund's eyes, forgot his doubts, and could not help saying yes to whatever she asked of him. Serving her would surely please St. Martin, whose shrine he could visit before going south to Burgundy. That way he could thank two saints at once, both Martin and Radegund.

When the poet had agreed to write and deliver the letter to King Guntram, Radegund offered him goat cheese on bread she had made with her own hands. She did not share the meal, but watched him thoughtfully as he ate.

"What is that ring you wear?" She asked, pointing at the ring of Pythagoras. "It has a power about it that gives me chills."

Fortunatus paused, a piece of bread halfway to his mouth, then said, "It came from a Greek holy man and philosopher who lived hundreds of years before Our Lord was born. Those who passed it on to me thought it brought power with it, as you say. I like to believe it brings wisdom also."

"Power and wisdom are seldom partners," Radegund smiled. "I think this ring might draw the wearer into one or the other, but not both. Guard yourself well, my friend, lest you follow an unholy path."

After he left the abbey and proceeded on to Tours, Fortunatus thought about her words. *The ring is a circle, closed upon itself, complete in itself. It contains, but it also excludes. The cross Radegund wears is open, pointing everywhere, embracing everyone, including everything.* He understood what she was telling him, that he must choose his path and not drift as he had all his life. *Wisdom or power. Which is it to be?* He thought of Radegund's white hands, of her luminous eyes, and of her bubbling laugh. Before he thought more about her than was good for his peace, he decided to visit St. Martin's shrine at Tours. He would thank St. Martin for the gift of sight which allowed him to see the beauty of Queen Radegund. To see more of her he dared not ask, for he feared surrendering that part of his soul she had touched.

Tours was not so much a city, Fortunatus thought, as an extension of the cathedral where the bishop dispensed alms and justice to the cluster of workmen and farmers whose huts dotted the area around the church. Fortunatus tried not to be critical of the ugly little place, with its pretension to cityhood and its homely reality. After all, it was the blessed site of the saint who had cured his blindness. The poet's fine dark eyebrows came together in a frown as he stood on the hillside overlooking the town where St. Martin had ruled and served. The great saint's cathedral was only a rounded stone edifice, towering over the huts, to be sure, but without the graceful arches that made the church of San Vitale in Ravenna a feast for the eyes.

Fortunatus had envisioned a better home for the relics of St. Martin, but knew by now that his expectations were based on foolish hopes. Vitale would have told him that he put too much faith in fine forms and too little in the spirit that shaped them. Fortunatus had missed his friend over the past year, which Vitale had spent serving the aged bishop of Tours. It had been too long since Vitale had urged him to visit Tours, and Fortunatus was glad that Radegund's errand had brought him to the shrine of the saint he needed to thank for his eyesight. Already he could feel the power of the saint's still living spirit pulsing from his relics in the cathedral, and the ring of power and wisdom burned on his finger in resonance with the saint's healing strength. *Perhaps Radegund's words about the ring should be heeded. It might be best to leave the ring on the tomb, as a gift for the saint. But no, my mission is to give the ring to one who would change the world. St. Martin has already done what he could do. Now it is up to King Sigibert and Queen Brunhild.*

At that moment, Fortunatus first began to think of giving the ring to Brunhild, who embodied royal power of the highest kind. In a way, it meant pledging himself to the world of the flesh, not the spirit, but he hoped that she could unite the two in the way Pythagoras had dreamed of. For a moment he imagined Radegund's bright gray eyes crinkling in amusement at his thought and wondered if she would say his hope was vain. Then he saw Vitale running from the cathedral and forgot about everything but how fine it would be to join his childhood friend and talk of old times and times to come.

"You must meet Gregory," Vitale said, after they had sat down at the dining table in the bishop's house. "He will someday be bishop here, I think, and a great one. I have asked him to join us."

Fortunatus was a little disappointed at the thought of meeting a stranger, however much he hoped that stranger would become a patron. He would need to behave himself and not get drunk. Sighing, he pushed his wine cup away.

"Tell me whose camp this Gregory is in," he said. "I don't want to blunder when I talk with him."

"He admires King Sigibert and despises King Chilperic," Vitale said. "You'll find him a man of aristocratic tastes and common, practical wisdom. I hope you'll be friends. Gregory is writing a history of the events that we are in the midst of. He will welcome your information."

Which I had best not convey, if I value keeping my head attached to my shoulders. Fortunatus only nodded, encouraging Vitale to go on.

"Gregory gathers information from everyone and puts it into his *History of the Franks*, as he calls it. *Historia Francorum*. Is that not a fine title? We aren't bereft of Roman culture here in Francia, as I promised you."

The door opened at that moment, and amidst a storm of coughing and gasping, Gregory entered. He was, as Fortunatus had heard, a diminutive man, with fine features and as bad a case of asthma as Fortunatus had ever encountered. Out of pity and concern, the poet rose to greet the sufferer and find him a comfortable chair.

"No matter," said Gregory between coughs, "Once I rest a little, all will be well. This late winter weather blows some ill wind that sends me into spasms."

Fortunatus felt his own lungs contract a little in sympathy as the man gasped and choked. "Haven't you asked St. Martin to cure you?" he ventured, wondering how it would feel to his air cut off, not knowing from one moment to the next if he could take another breath.

After sipping some water, Gregory seemed to breathe more freely, and smiled a smile so easy and kind that Fortunatus felt as if he had always known the man. "I've asked, but God sees fit to leave me with this thorn in my flesh," Gregory said. "It comes and goes, reminding me that I'm in charge of nothing, not even of the very air I breathe."

The men spoke of Fortunatus's sight being healed by St. Martin, and a little of the precarious state of Tours, hanging as it was between two kings, Sigibert and Chilperic. Vitale and Gregory feared for their small city, knowing that Chilperic could destroy it without a qualm.

"Chilperic is not a man to be trusted," Gregory said, taking a little food, but mostly talking. "He makes a vow easily and breaks it even more easily. His woman, Fredegund, is worse yet. Together, they plot to take all Francia and make us their slaves. I fear for the Church, if this godless pair succeeds."

"I think King Sigibert and his queen will have something to say about that," Fortunatus hesitated, not wanting to reveal too much about his mission.

He stopped talking and downed a glass of the surprisingly pleasant wine that Gregory told him was made from grapes grown nearby, along the River Loire.

"What would they say, do you think?" Gregory's sharp eyes studied the poet as if he already knew the secret Fortunatus carried. "Feel free to speak. Vitale will tell you that if I promise secrecy, I'll honor that promise. I'm no oath-breaker like Chilperic. Be sure of that."

After more wine and conversation, Fortunatus revealed his mission. Gregory promised to write a letter to Guntram urging him to follow Queen Radegund's advice. The poet and the historian were still talking when Vitale rubbed his eyes and begged to be excused for sleep. It was not until the middle of the night that their conversation died away.

"Gregory, I would like you to hear my confession," Fortunatus said, his voice unsteady. "Somehow, I think you'd understand what I've done, and what I've failed to do."

"I will hear you, my son," Gregory said, the words sounding strange to Fortunatus, since Gregory was hardly older than himself.

Still, the priest had an air of authority that made confession easy, and Fortunatus always appreciated what was easy. He sank to his knees in front of the little priest and told him about the sin with Phoebe and the two children resulting from it. Tears stood in his eyes as he thought of Agnes. The child had deserved more from him, and so had Phoebe. His tears fell freely, perhaps because of wine, perhaps because his own heart had been suddenly pierced by awareness of that blinding, selfish sin that had marred his youth.

"Phoebe was a slave in my household," Fortunatus whispered. "She had no choice, but I did."

"Fortunatus, dear son," Gregory said, holding out a hand over the poet's head and making the sign of the cross. "You have a good heart, despite your lapses, and God wants all of it. For your penance, pray every day for this woman and her children, and vow a life of chastity from now on, as did our great St. Augustine. His sin was like yours, and he turned it to the glory of God.

You will do the same. Celibacy is the way for you, hard as it might be. Not for everyone, but for you, it is. I see your need for discipline and pray you will find the one who can guide you into mastery of your soul."

Listening to Gregory, Fortunatus had a flash of a woman's face, silvery eyes seeing into his heart, and quickly put it aside. Radegund could not turn his soul God-ward, he thought, for she was the very object of his desire. Not wanting to tell Gregory of his unworthy thoughts about the lovely nun, Fortunatus fell apart in tears and groans, unsure whether he was suffering from a surfeit of wine or of love for a woman impossible to win.

The next day, too early for the poet's comfort, Gregory and Vitale waked him. The rain from the night before had turned to sleet, which Fortunatus could see through the narrow stone window above the bed in his monk's cell. His toes were cold, and he pulled them up under the heavy fur coverlet someone had laid over him. He closed his eyes, willing his two friends to leave him to his dreams of Radegund's white hands and the gray shawl that wrapped her slender form.

"Up now, Fortunatus," Vitale said, pulling back the cover and slapping a wet rag against the poet's forehead. "We must be on our way south before the weather worsens."

"Did Radegund send you with no retainers? No supplies?" Gregory shook his head. "That blessed woman! Because she lives on nothing but air, she thinks others do too."

"Gregory has begged a few of the bishop's guards for the journey," Vitale said, tossing Fortunatus's clothes on top of the poet's bare, shivering body. "And horses carrying supplies. And me. The bishop has relieved me of my work for the time it takes to accompany you on your journey to Burgundy."

Snatching at his clothes to cover himself, Fortunatus said between chattering teeth, "My thanks, Gregory. Radegund has magicked me, I think. I came away from Poitiers with no thought in my head but her."

"Careful, my friend," Gregory wheezed painfully as he laughed. "You wouldn't be the first man to pine for Radegund and lose his peace. Remember that she's pledged to Christ Jesus. She'll love you with God's own love, but no other way."

"I know, I know," Fortunatus muttered, wrapping his wool tunic tightly around his cold body. "But in my dreams, I know only that I love her. There. I've said it and will say no more. Vitale, I'll thank you for that rag in your hand to wipe the sleep out of my eyes."

He grabbed the rag and dunked his head in the bowl of nearly frozen water that sat by his bedside. No more dreaming for him today. He had his lady's errand to run and would do it without his usual excuses and delays. As he and Vitale said good-by to Gregory, he did not let his friends know what he was thinking. What would the whirlwind little priest say if he knew that the man whose confession he had heard only last night was already imagining how he might spend the rest of his life with Radegund in her abbey? An occasion of sin, Gregory would say. Give up such a dream, or you will imperil your chastity and both your souls. *No, I would do her no harm*, Fortunatus said wretchedly to himself, *I want only to be with her.* And so, alternately teasing and fooling himself, as he did too often, the poet went on his way. If Vitale knew the reason for his friend's sad silence, he was kind enough not to mention it.

The two travelers found King Guntram in a good mood. He was counting the treasure that dead King Charibert's wife had brought. This woman, a mere shepherd's daughter, thought to marry another king, and offered herself to Guntram along with her late husband's gold. Wise in the ways of the world, the crafty Guntram urged her to come to him at once. The woman's carts still stood in Guntram's courtyard, but her treasure was safely stowed in his storehouse. Having hardly looked at the former queen who hoped to be his bride, Guntram told a few of his men to escort the woman to the convent at Arles, where they were to deposit her. Far more important things than a childless widow were on the king's mind, and he was eager to discuss them with these messengers from Queen Radegund.

"I am well pleased with my portion of Charibert's lands," Guntram said, offering his visitors a table laden with delicacies that neither had seen since the royal wedding. "I will have more cities than I can govern. It's a pity that they're scattered here and there amidst my brothers' cities, but that's the Meroving way. We must learn to live together, I say. Have a stuffed date, my friend? They've been brought to me all the way from the island of Malta."

The plump king waved lazily to a servant, who hurried forward with a silver bowl. Fortunatus took a handful of the dates; Vitale took only one.

"Your wish to live in peace is worthy of you, majesty," Fortunatus said after commending the fruit. "Queen Radegund sent me to urge peace. Now that I know you, I see she needn't have worried about your intentions. However..."

"However, the good queen knows that Chilperic will seize the cities of Tours and Poitiers that should have been Sigibert's, yes?" Guntram's gleaming little eyes, half-buried in fat, flashed from one of the envoys to the other. "I suppose she would like me to support Sigibert in getting them back."

"I couldn't have said it more elegantly." Fortunatus was glad that the King had such a shrewd grasp of the situation.

Guntram stroked the ends of his long mustache with fat, greasy fingers. "And if I don't want to get involved? Why shouldn't I let Sigibert and Chilperic finish each other off, wearing out themselves and their fortunes in the process?"

"It might profit you to choose a side," Fortunatus said, putting down the date he was nibbling. Suddenly the food did not seem as appetizing as before. "You can well imagine that King Chilperic might be tempted to take his brothers down and seize all Francia for himself in a bloody war. That's what Queen Radegund fears and wants you to prevent. It would please her to know that you'll think about this proposal and send me back to Sigibert with an offer of support."

Pursing his lips, Guntram thought for a moment, idly stirring his gravy with one finger. Then he nodded. "I don't need time to make this decision. You may tell Radegund and Sigibert, too, that I will do as they wish. Chilperic could never be trusted to make peace, now that his witch of a wife is in charge of him. I'll offer Sigibert my armies to prevent Chilperic from upsetting the balance of power. You have my word."

Fortunatus overcame his distaste and kissed the unclean hand that the king held out to him. The whole affair had gone more easily than he imagined, and he happily anticipated telling Radegund about his first venture into diplomacy. *Peace is assured for the time being*, he thought, as he left the king's banquet hall. *Yet Vitale and Gregory, now Guntram, too, have warned me to beware of Chilperic.* The Neustrian king, who once had no cities south of the Loire, now possessed lands that stretched as far south as Visigothic Spain, Brunhild's homeland. Even if Sigibert, with Guntram's help, took back Tours and Poitiers, Chilperic could win in the end. The Neustrian king, after all, could lie and cheat and oath-break his way to power in a way impossible for the idealistic Sigibert and perhaps even for lazy, gluttonous Guntram. Worrying that Fredegund was going to persuade her husband to get rid of his brothers and take all Francia for his own, the poet stirred uneasily in his cushioned chair, wondering what his own fate would be in a land ruled by the likes of Chilperic and Fredegund.

Back at Radegund's abbey, Fortunatus told the queen of his triumph and his doubts. She commended him for his diplomatic efforts and offered him a bowl of strawberries drenched in clotted cream. Then she told him she had a happy surprise for him. *A gift? I remember her saying she'd found some truffles.* Fortunatus wondered as he began to eat the berries.

"You have a visitor," Radegund said, laughter in her voice. "She's already a joy to my heart, and I know will be so to yours." She clapped her hands three times, and looked at the doorway, through which came a slight, gray-clad figure.

Fortunatus leaped to his feat, overturning his chair. "Agnes!" he cried. "How can you be here?"

He was caught between delight at seeing his gentle daughter again and fear that Radegund would despise him for his past. What would she think of his sin with Phoebe? Of his sending the girl away with their two children? Radegund would believe him to be a monster. Someone so pure would know him for a lecher and a hypocrite. What had Agnes told Radegund, anyway? Had she complained of her father's abandonment of his family? Suddenly Fortunatus knew that his heroic act of self-sacrifice in sending Phoebe away was the work of selfishness, not renunciation. He thought of St. Augustine, leaving his woman behind and taking their son away from her. *At least I did nothing as cruel as that. There I go, excusing myself as always,* he admitted inwardly, *and daring to compare poor, foolish Fortunatus to the greatest saint of the church. I have to be honest, at least with myself and God. All right, I will be. I sent Phoebe and Agnes away because I wanted to be free of any ties. There it is, Lord, like it or not.*

Fortunatus felt his face turn red even as he reached out to catch Agnes in his arms. *She is an icon of the union between Phoebe and myself,* he thought, giving way to tears he hoped Radegund did not see. *She is the sign that God has forgiven me. I will never abandon her again.*

"Dear child, you've grown so tall," he murmured, holding Agnes tightly, his cheek laid against the veil covering her head. "What of your mother? The baby?"

Agnes sat down beside him on the bench, with Radegund across the table watching first one of them, then the other. "My mother married an old Greek courtier, who took her for love, not for the gold she had brought with her. He had enough fortune of his own. He adopted me and the son my mother bore you, little Cosmas. For a year, I went to school and studied Greek, as mother wanted. Then..."

His daughter's eyes clouded over with tears, and Radegund came around the table to sit by her and stroke her hair, while Agnes described her mother's death. Fortunatus sat apart from them, his head in his hands as he heard how Phoebe had died, bearing a third child stillborn. *O God, my poor Phoebe, she would have done as well or ill with me, yet I sent her away. May light eternal shine upon her, lovely girl that she was.*

He remembered how Phoebe had held him and wept when his eyes began to fail. Never once had she blamed him for the troubles he had brought on her. If it hadn't been for him and his lust, she would still be comfortably settled in his mother's villa, still alive. Fortunatus stifled a groan and covered his wet eyes with one hand. He could have loved her more, had he only loved himself less. *Her death was my fault*, Fortunatus thought. *Phoebe might forgive me from her place in heaven, if I take care of Agnes as a father should.* He reached for the girl's hand, without turning his face to her and gripped it hard. *And the son I'll never see, now the son of another man, someone who cannot love him as a real father could. I might have truly fathered him as my father did me, given him the best of myself.* For the first time the poet knew the difference between making poetry and making a human being, and the enormity of the difference embarrassed him. His son might have been flesh between his hands, as Agnes was now, but would never be more to him than a name.

He mourned in silence as Agnes told them how her mother's old Greek husband had decided to make little Cosmas his heir. He then intended to marry Agnes, despite her youth, and the girl had run away, taking with her some of the gold her mother had given her for just such a need. Agnes had cut her hair short, dressed as a boy, and fled Constantinople for Francia, following the trail of her father.

It had not been hard, since everyone of importance seemed to know of Fortunatus and his poems. He had been staying at wealthy estates all over

Francia, regaling his hosts with praise poems and consuming prodigious amounts of their food and wine. Agnes had not told them who she was, only that she bore a message for the poet from his family. She had been given hospitality and even an escort, once she got as far as Tours. *Ah, Gregory*, thought Fortunatus. *It must have been Gregory who helped Agnes find me at Radegund's abbey.*

"I know what it is to be given to an old man," Radegund said, putting an arm around the girl. "I, too, ran away. Here, my dear Agnes, you will be looked after and loved. If you like, I will be your mother now."

Agnes wiped her wet eyes and smiled up at Radegund. "I could ask for nothing more than to stay at your side for all my life," she said. "Oh, but I forget my father's here now. What do you want me to do?" She turned to Fortunatus and waited.

"If God has drawn you to Radegund, I have nothing to say about it," Fortunatus said, looking away from her and from the queen. "I don't deserve to be called father, or determine your fate, since I've served you so badly."

"Enough of that," Radegund said briskly, pouring water in the poet's cup. "I think we will tell no one about Agnes's parentage. She's simply a girl I chose for convent life and will train to follow my path. Is that agreeable to you, Fortunatus?"

Relieved, but feeling the need for a stronger drink than she offered, Fortunatus nodded. "It's best no one know she is my bastard child," he said. "No need for scandal. I give her gratefully to your guidance. You wouldn't happen to have a little wine?"

"Gregory says you have a weakness for it." Radegund poured him more water. "But there is no wine in this house except the small amount reserved for the Blessed Sacrament."

"Ah, well." Fortunatus sighed heavily, seeing her point. "In this perfect place, water can seem like wine. Perhaps that's what the miracle at Cana was. The presence of the Lord was intoxication enough and the wedding guests, drinking water blessed by him, may have thought they were drinking the finest wine."

Radegund shook her head. "I think when Holy Scripture says the Lord made wine out of water, then that's what he did. It was no doubt easier than making good men out of bad ones, and he did that all the time."

Agnes yawned, then closed her eyes, drooping against Radegund.

"Daughter, you must be tired of our talk," Fortunatus said, leaning forward to kiss the girl on her forehead. "I've waived my rights as father, but can still give you leave to sleep."

"So," said the queen, when her new spiritual daughter had gone off to bed, "you have me to thank for another favor. And will you again give me your help?"

"Anything," Fortunatus said, polishing off the last of the strawberries. "Ask, and it will be my pleasure to say yes." Suddenly he realized that for the first time in his adult life, he was trusting another human being with his future. It felt even more dangerous than leaving Ravenna for the northern forests.

"I would like to ask the Emperor Justin in Constantinople for a fragment of the True Cross," Radegund said, her pale hand curving around the wooden cross she always wore. "Would you write a letter and perhaps send a poem with it that might convince him to give me such a relic? All Poitiers would be gladdened by this gift that is in your power to bestow."

Fortunatus composed a letter and a poem which touched the emperor's heart enough that he sent the sacred relic into the depths of Francia. Emperor Justin never knew that it was his aunt's defamer who asked the boon, only that a holy nun who had once been a queen wanted the relic to inspire her countrymen on the path of Christ.

Less than a year later, in 569, the emperor's gift arrived in Poitiers. Radegund could not go outside her convent to receive it, since she had vowed never to leave its walls except under a bishop's orders. So she sent Fortunatus out at the head of a crowd from the city, bearing banners, and singing the song the poet had created for the occasion.

"O tree of beauty, tree of light. . ." they sang, and tears sprang to the poet's eyes as he took the holy relic in its tiny jeweled casket from the hands of the Greek envoy. It would lie enshrined in Radegund's chapel as a sign of God's protection. She and Agnes would be safe because of him. The music from a hundred voices blended in his ears with the elusive sound of the Logos, of God's Word, which had come to him at a few high moments in his life, sounding like buzzing bees and ringing bells, making him tremble in ecstasy. For once, Fortunatus thought, he had done good service to those he loved, and because this service made him happy, he resolved to go on doing it. *Perhaps someday,* Fortunatus thought, *I will become that music and dissolve into the heart of Christ. Until then, I will do as my lady Radegund asks, for in her voice, I can hear God's.*

His opportunity to serve Radegund again was not long in coming. A haughty nun, Chlothild, rebelled against the rigorous rule of St. Caesaria of Arles, chosen by Radegund for the Holy Cross abbey. Even though Radegund herself lived in a simple, dirt-floored hut, eating only lentils, Chlothild wanted special treatment. While Fortunatus was trying to get the old baths functional once again, Chlothild and forty of the nuns she had infected with her fury tried to take over the convent.

After summoning the Bishop of Poitiers, unfortunately no friend of hers, Radegund called Fortunatus to come into the main hall where she intended to confront Chlothild and the woman's royal delusions. The bishop had already arrived, and stared disdainfully at Fortunatus, who looked like he had been doing exactly what he had been doing, digging out broken ceramic pipe from under the bathhouse. Dusting off his hands on his woolen trousers, Fortunatus saw that Chlothild, her face distorted with rage, was standing in the middle of the room, some of her nuns behind her. She was waving her arms as she bellowed her complaints.

"I am a king's daughter, and I should rule here, not this common servant, Abbess Leubovera." Chlothild said the abbess's name like a curse, and pointed at the poor woman, who cowered behind Radegund.

"King Chilperic's daughter Basina and I will no longer put up with these wretched meals, ragged clothes, and cold rooms you have imposed on us, Leubovera. And you, Radegund, who appointed this incompetent fool, you are even more to blame. We know you tell her what to do, though you pretend to be no more than a humble nun."

Fortunatus raised an eyebrow at the woman's claim to be a king's daughter. Gregory had told him that although Chlothild said she was the dead king Charibert's daughter, few believed her. She might have been a concubine's child, but no one could be sure even of that royal connection. Basina, on the other hand, was the real thing, a Meroving princess. The abbey, Gregory had warned, could well be taken over by Chilperic, if he thought his daughter was being disrespected, since such disrespect might be interpreted as contempt for Chilperic himself. Or, the king might feel guilty that he had let Basina be violated by his own men, years ago and thrown out of her home, along with her repudiated mother. Being related to Chilperic, or any Meroving, for that matter, was no guarantee of respect. Radegund had received and comforted Basina as a nun at Holy Cross abbey, where the young woman reluctantly decided to remain, despite the austerities she had to endure.

Basina got up from the bench alongside the refectory wall, stood beside Chlothild, and noisily cleared her throat. The princess-nun was pretty, but the scowl on her face had always made Fortunatus want to avoid her. Unfortunately, Basina often tried to sidle up to him and make conversation, so much so that the other nuns warned Fortunatus she had designs on him. Fortunatus had always laughed at the thought, but was not laughing now.

"Everyone knows that the poet and Radegund are lovers," Basina said in her shrill, nasal voice. "That's why she gives him extra food and starves us."

Some of the assembled nuns murmured, "Shame, shame, Basina," but only one, Agnes, leaped from her seat and spoke out against the woman.

"You're a liar," Agnes cried. "I'm with the Lady Radegund night and day. Never is she alone with the poet. It is I who give him food, mostly my own. Make what you will of that, you spiteful thing."

She and Basina glared at each other until the princess turned away. Fortunatus was surprised that his gentle daughter had been brave enough to shout down a royal woman twice her age. Neither I nor Phoebe was so bold in our youth. Where does this bravery come from? Fortunatus glanced at Radegund and knew the answer. It was she who had mothered the shy girl into a fearless woman who would speak the truth, whatever the cost. Radegund often said, 'Perfect love casts out fear.' Agnes's love for Radegund, Fortunatus reflected, must be perfect indeed. He wished as much for his own, but knew that what he felt for the queen was not altogether holy.

The bishop was not finished. "And what, Abbess, do you have to say in your defense? You are responsible for your nuns' health." He looked not at Leubovera, but at Radegund, as if he knew which one of the two were to blame for the convent's troubles.

Leubovera declared in a high, shaky voice that the abbey food was good enough, given the famine of the past year. "The rooms may indeed be cold," she acknowledged, "but this winter has been harsh, and the peasants needed our firewood to keep their children warm."

"We live in simplicity here," Radegund replied, in her rich, low voice. "If you wish to live as a queen, Chlothild, perhaps you should go back home."

"You know we can't," Chlothild said, her lips tight, deepening the lines around her mouth. "Our fathers threw us out. Girl children are useless to them."

"Then we seem to be at an impasse." Radegund spread her hands, as if in an attempt to offer whatever she had. Her hands were empty because all she owned had been given away. She had nothing left for these angry, unwilling nuns.

The bishop frowned at her, and Fortunatus longed to smack him. "The convent must have new leadership," the bishop said. "Leubovera, Radegund, you must find someone among your nuns more fitted to rule than either of you are."

Leubovera buried her face in her hands and sobbed. Clearly, she was not about to defend herself.

"Your grace," said Fortunatus said, stepping forward. "I have no position here, but you know I have the blessing of your colleague, Gregory, and the friendship of King Sigibert. I speak in their names, not my own. Let us review our situation. Queen Radegund has set up a rule for her nuns asking more than some can bear. The princesses have difficulty abiding by such a rule," he bowed in the direction of Chlothild and Basina, "and that is to be expected of women used to fine living. Perhaps they might be housed in the abbey's villa and given access to better food and warm baths, if, God willing, the pipes I've just fixed don't crack again."

Radegund was smiling behind one hand, and the bishop stopped frowning. Chlothild nodded and nudged her friend Basina, who then nodded also. The matter had apparently been settled to their satisfaction and the bishop's. When the room was empty, Abbess Leubovera wept in Radegund's arms, declaring that she was not fit to be head of a convent, but wanted only to retire to her little cell.

"Soon, soon, my dear sister," Radegund said, stroking the woman's cheek. "You've gone through too much. I shouldn't have asked it of you. Shall I train a new person to be abbess?"

Fortunatus wondered who the queen meant. It seemed obvious to him that Radegund herself should openly lead the convent, but he knew she feared the corruption that power brought with it.

"Oh yes, Mother Radegund, please." Leubovera buried her face against Radegund's shoulder. "I will serve anyone you wish."

"I think it will be young Agnes," Radegund said, avoiding Fortunatus's eyes. "She and I are one soul. Yes, I think the new abbess must be Agnes." She got up and threw another log on the hearth-fire that warmed the room.

Fortunatus wondered at her decision. *If my poor little Agnes is to be so burdened, I should stay here, at her side. These princesses will destroy her if they can, just as they've destroyed Leubovera.* It might be Radegund's plan to keep a closer hold on convent affairs by making a dependent girl Mother Superior, then giving orders through her. Be wise as serpents, but gentle as doves, the Holy Scriptures taught. Radegund might well be heeding that advice, since her attempts to give away her authority to Leubovera had come to such grief.

Seeming to read his thoughts, Radegund invited him to dinner, serving him delicacies she herself did not eat. "Fortunatus," she said when he had finished his meal, "Without you, the bishop would have eaten us alive today. If you would like to make the abbey your home, you might serve us as overseer. It's hard for me to say it, but we need a man to intercede for us with the outside world and help keep order within our walls."

"I could travel?" Fortunatus weighed the invitation, thinking that much as he loved Radegund, staying in one place forever might make him dull. "Entertain visitors?"

"You would have to. Many of the people in this kingdom send to me for help and advice. If I answered them all, I would have no time for God. As the new leader of the abbey, Agnes will need your support. And I want to retreat into a more solitary life. What do you say?"

She would mention my daughter. How can I say no, if she wants me to stay for the sake of Agnes? Do I even want to say no? Is this place not what I have longed for? Is this woman not the north star of my wandering life? Yet still he hesitated, knowing he did not want to commit himself, unsure that he could live in Radegund's austere abbey and so close to her uncomfortable warmth.

Mastering temptation was not as easy for him, after all, as mastering hexameters. If he failed, as he had so often in the past, Radegund would be disappointed in him. Thrown back on his limited inner resources, Fortunatus feared he might turn savage like Chlothild, or break down like Leubovera. Worst of all, his desire for Radegund might fill him with discontent over their inevitable separateness. He tried to imagine a lifetime of closeness to Radegund without the link of flesh on flesh, watching her from a distance, longing for more than she could give him. Even in imagination, the picture wrenched his soul.

"You know how hard it will be for me to be beside you without touching your hands, your face..." Fortunatus knew he was turning red with shame at his thoughts, and sweat sprang out on his forehead. "You must know."

Suddenly he was aware that the pain she proposed for him was his penance, the thing he had always side-stepped. This time he would not. *I will accept my cross,* he vowed, *and I will do it out of love for this woman who can accept no other kind of love.*

Radegund withdrew a little, since he had reached out to her, hardly realizing what he did. She rose from her seat and poured water on the hearth fire until it went out.

"We have a holy friendship," she said. "With God's grace, we'll keep it that way."

"It would mean a life without smoked oysters," he said, trying to make light of his struggle.

"I can get them for you, on occasion."

"And I suppose I could have no wine." Fortunatus scratched at the little beard he was trying to grow. Life without strong drink was a grim prospect.

"No wine," Radegund replied firmly, then smiled. "But you will be loved here, not with brief, earthly passion, but with divine caritas, as Jesus taught. Love, my friend, is the wine of God. If you don't know it yet, you will."

So Fortunatus delayed his plans to leave the abbey and spent a week making a tile floor for the hut Radegund had given him as a guest-house. On one wall he hung a large green silk banner, embroidered with flowers on a cross, created for him by Agnes. Radegund had a writing desk made for him, identical to hers, and Fortunatus kept it under his one window, through which he could see the herb garden and a flowering thorn tree. Practicing on his lap harp and writing his poems as the weeks went by, Fortunatus felt no urge to travel, except when Radegund needed him to run an errand.

Because Guntram had joined forces with Sigibert, the poet could be at peace, like the kingdom. Chilperic had backed down, knowing he could not fight both his brothers, and Poitiers remained Sigibert's. Chilperic had even decided to raise his moral status in Francia by marrying Brunhild's sister, Galswinth, a step people hoped would limit Fredegund's power.

Life seemed to move along like a quiet river, undisturbed by rocks or rapids. Helping Radegund write her ceaseless flow of letters to the outside world, mainly to Sigibert and Brunhild as they strove to overcome one fierce warlord after another, Fortunatus never found himself bored. He even learned to cook the vegetables Radegund grew in her garden, combining them with herbs and mushrooms until they pleased his palate. He was in the kitchen with Agnes, grinding an herb paste, when Gogo, his old friend from the days at Sigibert's court, came rushing in, red-faced and panting.

"I've accompanied Queen Brunhild here to confer with her sister, Galswinth. Radegund says you should be present at this meeting."

Fortunatus wiped his hands on a rag, leaving a trail of green paste. "I can't imagine what good my presence would do, Gogo," he said. "I've been afraid of trouble ever since I heard that King Chilperic had married Brunhild's sister. We'd best stay out of it."

"I think they want us as witnesses to their conversation," Gogo said, wiping his damp forehead with the back of his hand. "Queen Brunhild is sure her sister is in serious trouble and hopes to keep her from harm."

Fortunatus slipped his arm under his friend's and started down the long hall from the kitchen to the reception room on the first floor of the villa. "These matters are beyond us, Gogo," he said. "I know Radegund wants to keep the peace, but does Brunhild?"

They came to the door of the great hall and stood there, watching the three queens. It was impossible to hear more than a few words of what they said, but Fortunatus was able to make out the gist of it. Brunhild wanted her sister to fight against Chilperic's concubine, Fredegund, while Radegund urged the new queen to let her husband do as he pleased. Either way, Fortunatus thought, Galswinth would come to grief. She was no match for Fredegund. Galswinth was pale, tall, and thin, with a nose too large for her small, narrow face. Remembering the beauty of Fredegund, with her lush figure and face like a Greek nymph's, Fortunatus knew well who would win. Yet Brunhild continued to argue that her sister should fight for Chilperic's love.

Shaking his head, Fortunatus glanced at Gogo, who winced at Brunhild's words. The sisters had no understanding of a man's desire for such a woman as Fredegund. They thought that policy and good sense alone could command Chilperic's allegiance. Remembering Fredegund's round, warm body and full lips, Fortunatus could almost hear her high, tinkling laughter at the notion that honor would win and desire would lose.

"I think they're saying what they would like to believe," Gogo whispered, "Not what is likely to happen."

"Radegund's probably right," Fortunatus replied. "She was married to Chlothar, and knows what a Meroving husband is like. I think that in this instance, she's the one with more practical wisdom."

"I know Brunhild," Gogo said. "She'll get what she wants, whatever the cost."

Radegund said no more to the other queens, but sent Fortunatus back to Metz with Brunhild. She whispered to him to stay there a while because she had a feeling that Brunhild might need him more than the convent did.

Reluctantly, the poet packed a change of clothes and his harp in a leather bag and saddled Glory, Radegund's horse. He planned to turn around and head for home as soon as he delivered Brunhild to her husband, since he could not imagine what the queen would need in the way of help from him. Already, he was longing to be home in his little hut, writing poems for Agnes and Radegund.

No sooner had he come back from Metz to the convent, having seen Brunhild safely home, then Radegund summoned him. He found her beside the hearth fire, her head in her hands. When she looked up at him, he saw that her cheeks were wet with tears.

"Galswinth is dead," she told him. "I think Fredegund killed her, but no one knows."

Fortunatus wiped his travel-stained face with the back of his hand. "You feared this would happen. Is that why you wanted me to stay with Brunhild?"

Rocking back and forth in her grief, Radegund said, "I had a sense of it, perhaps. It would not be the first time I guessed what was going to happen."

The poet sat down on the floor beside her, thinking of Brunhild and her sister in their last embrace. "Then I should have stayed at the court, as you told me to. Forgive my disobedience, Radegund."

"You owe me no fealty, my friend. But I thought you could be of help in preventing a war, as you have been before."

"I'll go back now." Fortunatus stood up and grabbed a bit of bread and cheese from the table. "This time, I'll stay in Metz until you call me home." He worried a little as he made this promise. Once he was gone, Radegund might forget all about him. But he was determined not to fail his queen again.

Radegund's informant at Sigibert's court had warned her that the rage of Brunhild was like a storm that threatened to drown the whole kingdom. The news spread fast. Peasants began to store food in the city and cultivate friends who might shelter them there, in the event of a siege. Soldiers looked to their weapons, and the blacksmiths' forges burned day and night turning out horseshoes and swords.

Fortunatus set out for Sigibert's court, riding Glory, the abbey's only horse. He left his new home with a heavy heart. A spring rain poured down on him, and he pulled his thick wool cloak over his head for protection. If war sweeps through Poitiers, he thought, Radegund will not be safe from Chilperic's savage soldiery, and even Gregory in Tours might see his city sacked and burned.

Gregory never failed to stand up to Chilperic, chiding him for his cruelty and even jeering that the king's verses staggered on lame feet. Chilperic would mind the last criticism more than the first, Fortunatus thought, and worried for his frail, brave friend. Fredegund had deprived her enemies of hands, ears, and tongue for less than what Gregory regularly said from the pulpit of the Tours Cathedral and in the letters he wrote all over Francia, making sure the world knew that Chilperic and Fredegund were enemies of God. What poems or soothing words of mine could protect the people I love, Fortunatus wondered, letting Glory stop to graze by the side of the rutted, muddy road.

He was in no hurry to get to the court he had so recently returned from. Radegund's last words to him rang in his ears, and as she said them, her eyes shone with unshed tears. Agnes had embraced him, but Radegund only stood still, her hands folded over her cross. The poet knelt for her blessing, and as he rode away, repeated it over and over, not wanting to forget the words.

"Christ Jesus, let us bring your peace to the warring princes, as you have brought it to our hearts." Radegund said. "And here is your message to the kings, Brother Fortunatus: 'Beloved, let us love one another: for love is of God. Everyone that loves is born of God and knows God. Blessed are the peacemakers, for they shall be called God's own children.' Amen."

Her voice sang the words into his soul, and Fortunatus went on his way, graced by the blessing and the after-image of its giver. Suddenly he understood that the Logos was not just a word but a song. *The divine music never ceases,* he realized and wondered at, *but we hear it only when our hearts open in love. Then the music plays us and we dance this truth. That must be what heaven is. May I someday be that music, not just sing it with my mouth.*

His heart too full for silence, Fortunatus took a deep breath and sang the name of Radegund over and over, with such a wild resonance that his whole body shook. When he stopped singing, echoes and overtones hung in the air like mist after rain. His horse turned its head, listening. Fortunatus forgot who he was and where he was going, for once without plans or future. Instead, he drank the moment and was filled. The first birds of spring sang in the treetops and the boughs were sleeved in a soft yellow-green that promised a new life, for the earth and for him as well. Kings and kingdoms were in the hands of God, not his. Content to have it so, the poet was at peace.

*Not by might or power but by
My Spirit," says the Lord Almighty.
Zechariah 4:6*

*"Who lives by the sword will perish by the sword."
Matthew 26:52*

Book II
The Warrior
Queen Brunhild

552 A.D.

Brunhild, daughter of King Athanagild was her father's favorite, the youngest and most brilliant of his children. He had allowed her to be educated and to sit at his side as he conducted the business of his realm, Visigothic Spain. From her earliest years, Brunhild had been aware that Hispania was under threat from outside forces. Once those forces had been her family's own, when the Visigoths swarmed down from the northeast in the year 409, taking over the whole land, except for the mountainous north coast where the Vascones hung onto their ancient, pre-Celtic ways. One of those ways was mother-right, going back to stone-age times, when the great goddess was venerated and women ruled alongside men, often over them.

The young princess was delighted with this practice of the Vascones and wished she could have lived in those long-ago times. Her older brother often taunted her, saying she should have born a boy because she wished so much to be king. The prince resented his younger sister's fluency in Latin, as well as her ability to get what she wanted from their father or anyone else. Once Brunhild had set her mind on something, no one could stop her, for she had a will of granite and a temper like the fabled volcanoes of Sicily. If she had not been a princess and beautiful, she would have been disciplined by the stick, like any other girl, but Brunhild, her brother said, would probably break the stick over the head of the man who tried to use it. "God pity your husband," he used to say.

But their father just laughed and went on indulging the daughter who charmed him with her sharp tongue and dimpled smiles. She would be a queen, she insisted to anyone who would listen, and she would rule as women had ruled in the days when men venerated the great goddess. Awaiting her chance for glory, Brunhild studied the history and politics of imperial Rome as they shaped the separate nations of Hispania, Gallia-Francia, and the hegemony of Byzantium, or Constantinople, as it was now called. She would study and learn, she told her older sister Galswinth, who smiled at the younger girl's passion for power, and someday, she would rule, as those in her family had before her. But she would create a world worth living in, like the one Augustus had ruled in the high, fine days of old Rome.

As Brunhild grew up, enjoying Roman baths, amphitheaters, and palaces, she learned she had nothing but physical appearance in common with the barbaric, German-speaking northerners. She belonged to the Roman culture of Hispania and prided herself on her ability to speak and read classical Latin. Her father had been ashamed of his illiteracy and had his children taught by Latin tutors brought from Rome. Brunhild excelled at all her studies but music, for she could sing only in a monotone. She read history with special care, determined that she would make her mark on it.

At the time Rome brought in the Visigoths to police Hispania, it had been an imperial province for seven hundred years and the birthplace of emperors and senators. Merida, the Roman capital, had fallen to one of Brunhild's ancestors in 483. Visigoths ruled under the regency of the Italian Ostrogoth, Theodoric, until Theodoric died in 526, two years after executing Boëthius. One weak king followed another, as Roman Spain fell apart in civil wars, her economy and aristocratic estates in ruins. The bubonic plague that swept through the empire in mid-century had brought depopulation, labor shortages, and civil chaos with it, weakening the central government still further. Brunhild absorbed these melancholy events with the knowledge that she must learn from them or repeat them in her turn as ruler. A strong central government was essential, she gathered from recent history, as was an imperial court that could control mangy, illiterate warlords whose hair smelled of bear grease.

Because Hispania was divided by mountain ranges and the rivers that flowed down from them, it was impossible to govern it as a single unit. Not only was the country fragmented by language and culture, but by religion. The Vascones in the northwest now called their mother goddess Magna Mater Maria. Catholics were scattered through the country, where they were persecuted by the Arian majority, who had been converted by the Goths. Because of Justinian's conquests, many civilized city people on the Mediterranean coast spoke Greek and followed the way of the Monophysites, seeing Jesus as God only, not man.

Brunhild was the heir of all these religious factions, and wanted to sort out for herself who Jesus really was. She talked more about it to Galswinth, her older sister, than to anyone. Galswinth was a serious young woman, who thought she might have become a nun, if the Arian church had had convents. Galswinth was protective of her younger sister and wanted to be sure Brunhild did not fall into lazy, sensual habits, as had so many of the noble women in Merida.

"I've given the matter much thought," Galswinth told Brunhild as they curled up together in their shared bed, not long after King Sigibert of Austrasia in northern Francia had sent an emissary inviting Brunhild to be his bride. "And I believe the truth lies somewhere between the Monophysites and the Arians."

"You mean that the Catholics have it right," Brunhild said, burrowing deeper under her fur coverlet. "That Jesus was both God and man?"

"I can't understand how that could be," Galswinth replied, "but my heart tells me Jesus brought heaven and earth together, and was not limited by one or the other. In him flesh and spirit were married to each other."

That night Brunhild dreamed of Jesus. At first he was just a kindly, polite man, then suddenly he became luminous, then transparent, then tall as a mountain. His voice was music that even she, tone-deaf as she was, could hear, as she heard the ringing thunder of church bells. Brunhild took the dream as a sign that her sister had been right about the Catholic view that Christ was mysteriously both God and man, however hard that was to believe.

Once Brunhild had determined which belief made sense to her, she accepted it and moved on. To her, a belief was not as important as the power it conferred. The Catholics of Francia had united their kingdom under their religious banner, and that was enough for Brunhild. The dream of Jesus faded from her mind.

When the invitation came from King Sigibert of Austrasia, a kingdom in the northeast of Francia, for her to be his bride, Brunhild knew she would find it easy to become a Catholic, like her husband. *Galswinth was right, as always,* Brunhild reflected. Without her sister, she wondered if she would forget about religion, since Galswinth's presence was all that kept Brunhild from being a slave to her royal ego. But then, religion had never absorbed her as had history and politics. When she was old and had nothing else to do, Brunhild figured, she might take up religion. Just now, she had more compelling matters on her mind.

King Athanagild had consulted with his daughter before giving his consent to the northern king. He had her brought into his conference room and seated on the same fur-decked stone bench where King Sigibert's representative had sat.

"You are of an age to be married, daughter," he said, taking her hand in his. "A great king has asked for you. I hear he is young, barely thirty, and well-favored. What do you say to this marriage?"

"Do we know anything about his family?" Brunhild asked, wanting to show her father that she was no child, but a prudent woman, well in control of herself. Still, a voice inside her spoke an unsettling thought. Her life was at a crossroad. If she married in her father's kingdom, she could rule her husband. Once she chose to leave Spain, she might never again be able to set her own course. Brunhild felt a chill run down her back at the thought of not being her own mistress.

"His older brother Chilperic has several wives, if they can be called such," Athanagild said. "Sigibert wants no mere liaisons—just one wife. He is said to be a man of integrity, living his religion, unlike his brothers. But I must tell you, my dear, I fear these Merovingian kings. They've earned a name for treachery and infidelity. I don't know if we can trust them."

Brunhild closed her eyes and took a deep breath. She knew that Galswinth would not advise her to give herself lightly. Yet something about what her father said of King Sigibert resonated in her like the strings of a harp when touched by a master's hand.

"Father, I know that Francia is a barbaric place, but Sigibert is no barbarian, I hear. We should say yes to him. I think this is my destiny."

"Before you decide," King Athanagild said, "Talk to Gogo, his emissary. I have arranged your meeting with him tomorrow morning. Ask him what you wish. Your mother and I have sworn not to marry you against your will. Marriage can be a terrible thing for a girl or a great joy. We want it to be a joy for you."

So the next day, small, toga-garbed Gogo met with the princess his king sought in marriage. He was nervous and waved his hands in the air as he talked, trying to show this tall, frowning princess who was in charge of the interview.

"My prince is a man favored by God, taller even than you are and just as handsome." Gogo said before Brunhild could even sit down on her chair.

"He seeks a woman who is similarly favored. I am sent to learn if you are the one he should marry."

"That leaves little of the decision to me," Brunhild murmured, trying not to smile at the little man's posturing and lunging about, as if he were a soldier with a sword. "Tell me, how are his teeth?"

Gogo paused in his gyrations. "His teeth? Well, he has all but one. A battle with a Thuringian knocked out a side tooth. But the rest are intact. He has a generous smile, lady, and would please a queen."

"He will have to," Brunhild nodded. "And he has no concubines?"

"Sigibert is not like his brothers. He wishes only for a queen who would grace the Austrasian throne. He wishes for you, Lady Brunhild."

"You say he is taller than I am," Brunhild mused, half to herself. "That's promising, I think. And does he scold? Beat his dogs? Tell me about his temper."

Gogo relaxed into a smile. "Princess," he said, "Sigibert is a man of sunny temperament, good-natured to all, except those who betray him. His dogs lie in his lap and his friends never fear to approach him."

"I accept him, then. Dogs are the finest judges of character, more so than friends. As we go north, you will instruct me in Sigibert's language and his faith. They shall be mine, whatever their oddities. Let the marriage take place as my father wishes."

Thus it happened that Brunhild said good-by to her parents, and her sister, Galswinth, was left weeping, as the royal entourage, laden with a dowry befitting a queen, went north along the banks of the Guadalquivir. Brunhild had no urge to weep and could not wait to say good-by to the land her forebears had so recently conquered. North was the direction for her, back to the snows and dark forests of her ancient ancestors. The princess was content and smiled at Gogo when he tried to explain to her what Sigibert believed. *Be Christ man or God, it's all the same to me,* Brunhild told herself, for she did not want religion to turn her otherworldly. Having decided on her creed, she would leave doctrinal matters to priests and to thinkers like Galswinth. Becoming a Catholic would make her a queen acceptable to her subjects, and only that now mattered to her. She was sixteen, beautiful, and rich. Sometimes she felt that she could control even God himself.

On the way through Francia, Gogo lectured the princess on the central Catholic belief, unlike what she had learned as an Arian. "God is not only One, like human beings, but Three in One." Gogo started to wave his hands about and almost fell off his horse.

Brunhild decided to show him that she needed no instruction in this matter. She was about to become a queen and could think for herself. "God is beyond our understanding," she said to him, brushing away the flies that buzzed around her face whenever she spoke. They seemed to like the tone of her voice and vibrated insistently with it. "A human, after all, is just one being. God would have to be more than what we are. I think the Three means God is such a mystery that no mind can comprehend him but his own."

Gogo stared at her, pulling at the shoulder-piece of his toga, which tended to slip down over his arm. "Just so, my lady. You're a philosopher, I see."

"Not at all," laughed Brunhild, "Just a curious, practical woman. Gogo, you can tell your king that you have converted me and that I will be baptized in the Roman way when I meet him in Metz. That should please both him and you."

Gogo was indeed so pleased that he spent the rest of the trip haranguing Brunhild on Catholic theology. She smiled and nodded, but her mind was occupied with the sight of snow melting into rushing streams and with thoughts of Sigibert. His face would be smooth, with a strong jaw. No, he would wear a golden mustache, and a thick short beard would cover his cheeks and chin. At last she decided to imagine nothing, lest the reality fail to match her dreams.

By the time she reached Metz, Brunhild wanted only to rest and lie in a luxurious, warm Roman bath, soothing her aching muscles. The best that a local convent could provide was a tub no bigger than a chamber pot, in which she was expected to wash first her face, and then, one by one, her dusty limbs, finally her long, grimy locks. *Sigibert will think I smell like a pig,* Brunhild said to herself as she set to work. *Holy God, they use ash for soap.* She called for another pot of water, then another, until at last her hair squeaked clean under her fingers. Galswinth had given her a parting gift of jasmine essence which she used to scent her armpits and her hair. It would have to do. Given the local standards of hygiene, surely Sigibert would likely smell no better than she.

The royal pair was to meet only once, just before the parade to the church. Brunhild was determined not to convey a false, womanly mildness. *First impressions tend to be lasting ones. I want Sigibert to understand from the start that I am his equal.* More than that, if she could manage it, but equal at least. She wore a red silk robe over a purple silk gown that fell from her neck to her toes. Only the highest classes were permitted to wear silk, especially silk that was dyed purple, so Brunhild was making a statement by the clothes she had chosen. The robe was wrapped tightly under the bosom and flared over her hips, showing off the slenderness of her waist. On her head, she wore a long indigo veil that fluttered over her hair and was held in place by a lavishly jeweled gold circlet. She meant Sigibert to know she was a queen already.

Having given so much thought to her own appearance that she forgot about Sigibert, she was startled at the sight of the young king, who stood at the entrance of the convent and called her name in a deep, ringing voice that unstrung her heart.

"Sigibert, I'm here," she said, walking through a stone archway toward him, holding out her hand, low enough that he would know he was to kiss it in homage.

Instead, Sigibert held it and drew her close to him, looking down into her face. "You're all you were said to be, princess. I'm glad to take you as my queen."

He smiled, and Brunhild saw only the dimple on one cheek, not the gap where he had lost a tooth. She reached up and touched his long blond mustache, then his smooth-shaven cheek. "You are what I imagined a king to be," she said. "We will suit each other well."

Sigibert's thick blond hair was longer than hers, for it had never been cut since his birth. No king of the Merovings could be shorn, lest his power be stripped from him, and Sigibert wore his hair like a cape spread over his broad shoulders and back. Strangely, Brunhild thought, the wild, uneven locks made him look even more a man than short hair could. He looked to her like a god out of the northern legends, ready more for battle than a wedding.

All thought of dominating this man, whose shining blue eyes were so like hers, had fled from Brunhild's mind. She loved him at first sight and knew he had only to command her for her to do his will. At the same time, she knew she had only to command him, and he would do hers. They were one heart and soul already, truly married even before the words were said in church.

"My whole life long," Sigibert said, as he led her to the cart in which she would travel to the cathedral, "I will love no woman but you. God meant us for each other, beloved. Can you feel that, as I do?"

Not waiting for an answer, he lifted her into the flower-decked cart, and his hands lingered on her waist in a way that made her cheeks turn warm. She followed Sigibert's cart through the crowd, wishing they had been driving chariots in the Roman style. People called out her name in praise and tossed flowers before her horse. For a moment she thought of Christ entering Jerusalem with palms thrown down before him, but turned her mind away from that image, remembering what happened afterward on Golgotha. Best to stay in this fine moment, she thought, wishing Galswinth were there to see the size of the Metz Cathedral. True, the statuary was not the best, and timbers could never be as beautiful as stone, but in time, she would bring Italian and Spanish sculptors north to do the work as imperial Romans would have done it. The rough, cobbled road would be made straight and smooth, once she was queen, and chariots would replace the rustic carts.

Sigibert glanced back at her and smiled his dazzling smile, turning her knees weak. His broad shoulders and bulging upper arms almost burst from his leather tunic. *This Sigibert is a warrior*, she said to herself, *and while he fights his battles, I will rule at home, turning this rough place into a new Rome, bearing sons who will carry our name and blood into the future Francia.* The sons of Chilperic, standing behind their father, would surely not dare to oppose her offspring. The oldest one appeared sickly, and Merovech, the younger one, was delicately handsome, a dandy who probably cared more for his clothes than for weapons. Brunhild could not help noticing that Merovech looked at her with a passionate stare she would not have thought possible for such a young boy. She had no objection to being admired and tossed him a slight smile. *This fellow might be useful*, she thought. *To have an ally in King Chilperic's household might prove very useful indeed.*

The wedding itself passed in a blur, the words of the bishop were no doubt sacred, but to Brunhild, they were nothing. Yes, she needed the bishops and the church, but it was Sigibert and she who made the marriage and ruled the realm. As they left the church, Sigibert held her close to him, so that no one could doubt they were already one.

He made each of his relatives known to her. First, there was fat, agreeable Guntram, his favorite brother. Then came Charibert, a sly-looking fellow with a weak chin and watery eyes. She had heard stories about the nuns he had lured into his bed and about his unhealthy habits. *This one won't make old bones*, Brunhild surmised, dismissing the oldest of Sigibert's brothers with a distant smile. At the end came Chilperic, a slender, sensitive-looking man of medium height, who had to look up to meet Brunhild's eyes.

"I greet you with joy, sister," Chilperic said, his voice somewhat high and unmanly. "You grace the word queen with your beauty." He spoke in Latin, showing off.

Brunhild nodded and extended her hand, which Chilperic kissed with lingering, moist lips. "My husband's kin are mine," she said noncommittally.

"Be pleased to meet my. . .wife, Fredegund," Chilperic said, pushing the cat-faced little woman forward.

In repose, the woman's countenance was beautiful, with high-cheekbones, wide spaced dark eyes, and full red lips, a face assisted by considerable art. But when Fredegund smiled, she looked like an animal ready to eat its prey. Brunhild stepped back and quickly withdrew her hand from Chilperic's, lest he give it over to his so-called wife. Gogo had explained that Fredegund was only a concubine, but here she was, parading at Chilperic's side as if she had a wife's right to be there.

"I cannot recognize you as a sister, Fredegund," Brunhild said stiffly, turning to Sigibert for support.

Fredegund stepped back too, her eyes and cheeks blazing. "You'll suffer for your pride, princess," she said, in a high, piercing voice. "I don't take insults lightly."

"Yet insults are what you're likely to get," Brunhild could not help replying. "At least from me."

Sigibert took his bride's arm and guided her outside into the sunlight. "That was unlucky, beloved," he said. "Fredegund is dangerous. We must not offend her, for she commands my brother Chilperic in all things."

"He should learn from you, Sigibert," Brunhild replied, "and get a wife worthy to command him."

In time these words came back to haunt Brunhild. Not long after, she heard from her mother that Galswinth was coming north to become Chilperic's wife. The girls' mother knew of Chilperic's bad reputation and was frantic with worry. She had tried to stop Athanagild's plan for yet another Frankish alliance, but her husband was adamant. Had not Brunhild found marriage to Sigibert a blessed union? Perhaps Galswinth would win Chilperic's heart, too. Brunhild trembled for her sister, knowing that Fredegund would not accept replacement without a fight.

As she and Sigibert lay late abed one morning, twined in each other's arms, Brunhild told him of her fears.

"Galswinth wrote to me," she said, pulling the linen cover up over them both. "She's settled into her new role as queen. It wasn't easy for her, I know."

"And how goes it with my brother and your sister?" Sigibert rolled over on his stomach and looked into her face. "If she's anything like you, he must be in love."

"She's nothing like me," Brunhild answered. "Galswinth never thought to be married, thin and ill-favored as she is. No suitors asked for her, despite her wisdom and kindness. They're the poorer for it. Sigibert, I fear that sly cat, Fredegund."

"My brother's a fool for pretty women," Sigibert nodded, "but he's also a fool for money. Galswinth brought with her a fine dowry and cities in the south worth more than all my brother's holdings. He'll have to treat her well. Look at the morning-gift he gave her the day after the wedding. Five of his best cities, not that they're as splendid as hers, but still. . ."

"And if he doesn't treat her well? Will you protect her? She's far from my father's help, and he never loved her as he did me."

Sigibert laid his head on the pillow of her thick, fragrant hair. "If you ask anything, I will grant it," he said. "But let's hope that Galswinth is well and happy."

"Then why would she want to meet me at Radegund's convent?" Brunhild felt a sudden chill and pushed her body close to Sigibert's.

Sigibert sat up and stared at her. "You can't be thinking of travel. Not in your condition." He rested one large, gentle hand over her slightly swollen belly.

"I'm only four months' with child," Brunhild said, "and Poitiers is not so far away from here. Your Greek physician says I'm in good health and that this short trip should do me and the child no harm." Throwing one arm around his neck, she pulled his face close to hers.

"Galswinth is my only sister, dear one. I must go to her if she needs me, as I would go to you."

Sigibert at last gave in, as Brunhild had known he would, but insisted that she be accompanied by the royal physician as well as fussy little Gogo, and a small army of his most trusted men. Gogo would keep her company with his refined conversation. Sigibert would expect a letter from her every day and would not cease to pray for her return with every breath. And so Brunhild set out in a lavishly padded, covered cart, surrounded by her retainers. Only after they had left Metz well behind, did she commandeer a horse and ride at the head of the procession. After all, she thought, what Sigibert did not know would not worry him.

The Abbey of the Holy Cross was not imposing, Brunhild thought, as she approached the half-built stone chapel and the collection of small, thatched huts that surrounded it. At least an old Roman villa had remained to house important guests, she was glad to see. There might even be a bath and indoor toilets, if the villa had not been allowed to decay entirely. The soldiers set up their tents around the abbey, and Gogo guided his queen to the main door of the villa. He told her of his admiration for Radegund, about whom he had more to say than Brunhild cared to hear. She liked hearing her own praise, but was not keen on hearing praise of another woman. It made her feel as if she were wanting in some respect. She certainly had none of Radegund's high and mighty spiritual powers, not that such things mattered much to her. *The woman was a queen and is now a nobody,* thought Brunhild, *and of her own foolish choice.* Still, it stung a little to hear the man run on about what a saint Radegund was.

She was led into the Roman villa by Sister Chlothild, whom she knew claimed to be the daughter of King Charibert, though no one was sure by which concubine. Chlothild kept her face closed in a fastidious sneer, refusing to acknowledge Brunhild as royalty. Clearly, this large-featured, heavyset woman thought herself a rightful princess who had fallen on evil days. She did not speak to Brunhild, but merely gestured her and Gogo toward a door within the deteriorating house, leaving them to manage for themselves.

Galswinth had already arrived and sat on a Roman folding seat before the stone fireplace at the end of what had once been a banquet room. Radegund sat close beside her, one arm around Galswinth's thin, bony shoulders. Both women rose as Brunhild entered the room, followed at a discreet distance by Gogo. Fortunatus had joined him, and the two men stood near the door, as if on guard, while Brunhild ran forward to meet her sister.

"I forget myself," Brunhild said to Radegund, after releasing her sister from a fierce embrace. She bowed to Radegund. "Your majesty, it's my pleasure to meet you again. Many thanks for receiving my sister and me."

Radegunde gestured to a third chair. "I'm just Radegund, now," she said in a soft, velvety voice. "Treat me as your servant, for I wish to be so while you are here."

The woman did not seem at all like a servant to Brunhild, but more like a mother keeping her children close beside her as the three of them sat together.

"So, Galswinth," Radegund said in a kind but businesslike way. "We want to hear how it goes with you and your new husband. Nothing you tell me of King Chilperic would be a surprise, so you needn't fear to speak ill of him, if you must."

Her shoulders drooping in despair, Galswinth began to weep as she spoke, choking out her words. "He loves my fortune, not me," the bride said. "His concubine, Fredegund, all but spat in my face. She told me I wouldn't last and could never please the king the way she does. I got the feeling she wanted me to leave and go back where I came from. Without my dowry, of course."

Radegund stroked the young bride's tangled, mouse-brown hair away from the girl's wet eyes and cheeks. "Did she actually threaten you? Understand that Fredegund has killed other women who caught Chilperic's eye. She is no doubt jealous of your royal family, being herself only a poor creature, scarcely a step removed from slavery."

It occurred to Brunhild that Fredegund had perhaps been a slave or the daughter of slaves, since many such *servi* from the south and east had been sold to the Franks or captured by them. If Fredegund's family had been among such miserable folk, it was not hard to see why the woman might fear to lose her position as the king's favorite. Brunhild knew Fredegund had been a servant of the former queen and had never acknowledged being a slave. Of course, she would not, given her obvious pride.

"You must fight back," Brunhild said, her eyes blazing. "I would. This Fredegund has to be sent packing. Tell Chilperic that if he doesn't get rid of her at once, you'll return to Spain and take your dowry with you."

"Can I do that?" Galswinth stopped crying and looked at her sister as if she were some kind of divine oracle. "Will he let me? I so miss our mother." Her tears flowed again.

"Of course you can. You're a princess of royal blood. No one has the right to insult you, least of all this little cat bitch. Excuse me, Radegund, I call things as I see them. Face her down, my sister. If you wish, I'll send someone to cut her throat before she insults you again."

"Wait a minute," Radegund said, raising one slender white hand with an authority that silenced them both. "We'll have no talk of murder here. Two kingdoms are at stake, remember. Galswinth, a battle between you and Fredegund could result in many deaths, much suffering. Do you wish me to advise you?"

The wretched bride nodded, scattering her tears across Radegund's immaculate light gray cloak, so that little dark spots appeared on it. "Please. I'm not strong like my sister. Confronting others has always been painful for me."

"Then be yourself," Radegund said. "Accept the presence of Fredegund, knowing that once you bear Chilperic a son, he'll put Fredegund aside, or at least put her at a distance from you. His father was the same as Chilperic, having many women. I didn't fight him on that score. Galswinth, no man can be as dear as Christ Jesus. Hold the Lord in your heart and let men be what they wish to be. It's not your concern if their lusts carry them to women like Fredegund."

"Radegund, I can't agree with that," said Brunhild, leaning between the two women as if she hoped to break the connection between them. This talk of religion irritated her. *The issue here is queenship,* she thought. *Power. Radegund, having thrown away her own power with both hands, can't understand what's at stake.*

"My sister must fight for her rights. If she lets Fredegund win, she'll never have the son who would make her a queen indeed."

Brunhild remembered what Sigibert had told her of the woman who was plotting against her sister. Even in their youth, this servant of their mother had tried to seduce first one son, then the other. Sigibert had been repelled by Fredegund's attempts to slide into his bed. He knew she hungered for power, not for him. To Sigibert, she seemed old, too skilled in matters of the flesh. But Chilperic, being fourteen and lusty, found her delicious. He boasted to his brother of his wild nights with the young servant girl. When Sigibert objected that Fredegund might become pregnant and want to get married, his half-brother laughed, saying the girl knew how to prevent or destroy a pregnancy with herbs and spells. Sigibert had pretended to know all about such things, but ever since had feared Fredegund as a witch.

"What if Fredegund has a son before I do?" Galswinth hiccupped in the midst of her weeping, and Radegund held some water to the young woman's lips.

"So far she has prevented pregnancy," Brunhild said. "I think she means to hold Chilperic without risking her good looks."

"And I have no good looks to worry about." Her sister sat back, sighing. "Why would he favor me over her, even if I had a son? They would take him away from me and go on doing what they do now."

"You may be right." Radegund folded her hands in her lap and looked down at them. "Galswinth, whatever you decide, know that you always have a home here with me. The Lord receives his own and comforts them. Remember."

Brunhild's heart beat faster, for she knew the holy queen had lost the battle. What Radegund offered was only a hut and a cup of gruel, when Galswinth had been promised a kingdom.

"I'll tell Chilperic to send his concubine away," Galswinth whispered, keeping her eyes on her sister's. "You'll be proud of me, Brunhild. So will our family."

Riding back to Metz, all smiles in the gladness of winning, Brunhild asked Fortunatus to sing her a song about the beauty of old Rome. She did not know why Radegund had wanted him to accompany her, but thought the man might at least offer some entertainment. He complied with her request for a poem, although his mind seemed to be elsewhere.

Brunhild smiled at the thought of her sister becoming a real queen, a colleague in the re-creation of Rome in the northern wilderness of Francia. That night, resting in a bishop's villa, she dreamed of Roman baths and fountains, Roman amphitheatres and lavish productions of ancient plays. In her imagination, Rome lived again, and she saw herself and her sister creating a second, better Roman world in the cold, forested north—a Holy Roman Empire, this time one pleasing to God, who would certainly make it flourish.

The child stirred in her womb as she greeted Sigibert two days later. Fortunatus, before he left for Poitiers, had urged her to ride the last few hours, pillowed in her cart, lest she worry her husband. Brunhild reached out to Sigibert, and he lifted her down onto home ground. She could not understand why his face was grave, not happy like her own.

"What is it, beloved," she whispered, her lips against his cheeks. "Aren't you pleased to see me?"

"Come with me to our own chamber, love," he said, his arm around her waist, half-lifting her off the ground. "I have news you must hear in private."

Brunhild felt her dinner rise in her throat and shook as if hit by a fever. *What has he heard? Has Fredegund struck like the snake she is against my poor Galswinth? Is Galswinth even alive?* Without a word, she followed him to their chamber and let him carry her to their bed. For the first moments, he did no more than caress her, then he fell back on his pillow, one hand over his eyes.

"Husband, tell me, what is it?" Brunhild cried, pulling his hand away from his face.

"Your sister," Sigibert's voice was harsh and choked, as if he were going to be sick. "She's dead at Chilperic's hand. Or Fredegund's. It is the same."

Brunhild sat on the side of the bed and a scream rose from her throat, distorting her face. "Galswinth," she cried, her shoulders hunched over and her back frozen hard as if she lifted a weight heavy as a wooden cart. "How? Tell me everything."

"A messenger came just before you, riding hard," Sigibert said. "He said your sister is dead. We know nothing more."

Brunhild pounded her knees until they ached and screamed until her throat hurt. "That monster she married," Brunhild cried, the tears pouring down her cheeks, "that cat-bitch of his. They'll pay with their lives for what they've done to my sister. I swear it."

"Beloved, calm yourself. I feared this." Sigibert tried to stroke her back, but she leaped from the bed, prowling the room like a wild animal. "You'll turn the child sick in the womb if you go on so."

"My child will share my vengeance," Brunhild muttered, letting her mind dissolve in fury, caring for nothing but revenge. "Don't think to calm me, husband. We'll fight Chilperic and Fredegund until we cut them to pieces. Promise that you'll avenge me. Promise."

She screamed again, her face white and drawn, as if she were possessed by a demon. Brunhild kept on screaming until Sigibert held her down on the bed, promising to do anything she wished, if only she would stop screaming and injuring their child with her fury.

The next day, Sigibert sent for his brother Guntram and the two of them sat down to determine a strategy. Brunhild had taken to her bed, under the Greek physician's care, and lay quiet, weeping or sleeping according to the way the physician's medicines worked. Glad to know she was more or less at rest, Sigibert spoke to his brother.

"We must preserve the peace at all costs," Guntram said to Sigibert. "Your wife has every reason to be angry, but you must tell her to give it up to God. So Radegund advises me. If Brunhild insists on vengeance, many will suffer and die."

"I know, I know," muttered Sigibert, running his hands through his long hair. "But she's wild. I fear for her and for the baby."

"Brother, you know my children are dead," Guntram said. "Your children will be mine. Our childless brother Charibert is dead, so your sons will be heirs to our father's kingdom. That is, if we can keep Chilperic satisfied. Radegund thinks it is possible."

"Brunhild insists on fighting Chilperic to the death," Sigibert replied. "I'm sworn to avenge her sister."

"You and I will fight side by side, then," said Guntram, eating another date from his plate of sweetmeats. "And we'll win. Chilperic was always more a scholar than a general."

Sigibert agreed, letting his brother decide what to do. He was a warrior, after all, not a politician. If Chilperic had to be destroyed, so be it. It was, as he had long thought, his divinely determined destiny to rule Francia and turn it both Roman and Christian. Brunhild had told him her vision for their kingdom, and he was committed to it, as he was to her. His heart was at rest as he received the poet Fortunatus, who had been charged by Queen Radegund to keep the peace if at all possible. He had ridden all day, and his clothes were stained with sweat and dirt.

"I would like the lady Brunhild to tell me what kind of elegy she wants for her sister," Fortunatus said, after bowing to Sigibert. "Radegund wants peace, and tells me that an elegy referring only to Queen Galswinth's untimely death might help to keep tempers from being inflamed."

"You mean well, poet," Sigibert said, only half his mind on the conversation. "But I doubt that my queen will be comforted by such a thing. We well know who killed her sister."

"The noble Radegund says that we must not attack or blame King Chilperic for this tragedy," Fortunatus said, averting his look from Sigibert's reddened, angry eyes. "To blame him would be to bring about a fury of fighting and the suffering of all your people."

Before they could say another word, the curtain behind Sigibert's broad, leather- padded throne was flung aside, and Queen Brunhild entered the room. Her round cheeks were blotched with weeping and her voice was harsh with rage.

"Poet, I want you to turn my sister's death to verses that will never die," she said, sitting on Sigibert's lap, one arm around his neck. "But you must tell the truth. The murderers of my sister must be accused and destroyed."

"Please, great queen, let me tell you what Radegund recommends. And tell me everything about your sister and her life that you want immortalized. Then I'll write as you wish."

Sigibert seemed relieved as Fortunatus guided the grieving queen to a seat and took up his stylus to write. "I leave the two of you to find words of comfort," he said.

"And you, husband, what will you do?" Brunhild threw her head back and took a deep breath, as if she were about to weep again.

"I'll decide what must be done to Chilperic," Sigibert said. "Guntram will help me. I think we must fight my murdering brother, not just write about his crimes."

"Maybe fighting won't be necessary," Fortunatus said. "Let us try to reason together, my queen. Let us try to save the peace, as Radegund wishes. Shall we begin?"

As she sat listening to the poet sing the opening measures of his poem to Galswinth, Brunhild began to feel cramps in her belly that doubled her over. Fortunatus stopped singing in the middle of a line and stared at her ashen face.

"Lady, what ails you?" He let his harp slide to the floor. Rushing to Brunhild's side, he called for her servants, for Sigibert, for anyone within hearing. The king was in the room even before her women.

"The child," she gasped, hardly able to speak as her body seemed to rip in pieces, pouring blood out of her. "I'm losing the child. Sigibert, help me. . ." She fell into the king's arms.

Brunhild had no memory of Sigibert carrying her to their bed, nor of the passing of their dead child from her body. When she awoke, Sigibert was lying beside her. With one hand, she touched her belly, which curved inward again. The baby was gone, and they might never have another. *I might be one of those women who cannot keep a child in the womb, and no issue of mine will rule after me.* At this thought, Brunhild wept silently, not wanting to wake her husband. It might be that she had caused the baby's death by riding horseback against Sigibert's wishes. Or by the violence of her outburst when she heard of Galswinth's death. Or by the potions the doctor had been obliged to give her in order to calm her rage. Brunhild pushed such thoughts away, reminding herself who had been the real cause. Fredegund and Chilperic were to blame, no one else.

Later, in Sigibert's arms, she wept again and once more demanded the death of these enemies. They would pay for their crime, if she had to go to Neustria and kill them herself. Now there was one more death, her unborn child's, to lay at their charge. Fredegund and Chilperic must pay, she insisted. But if Sigibert promised he would destroy them, she would agree to wait for a little while. Sigibert soothed her with promises that their vengeance would come when the moment was right. Brunhild could only hope that moment would come soon.

Retaliation could not be immediate, in any case. Alliances had to be built and strengthened; nobles had to be bribed for their support; armies had to be trained and deployed in strategic places. Over the years of waiting, Brunhild and Sigibert's first child was born, Ingund, a girl, to the queen's sorrow. She wondered if God were punishing her for her anger and hatred, but surely, Brunhild told herself, her rage was justified. She had read in the Bible that even God could be made wrathful by human crimes. He would not blame her for wanting to carry out his justice on her enemies.

Then a boy baby was born to them, and Brunhild's spirits began to lift. God was with them once more, and would be on their side when the time came for punishing Chilperic and Fredegund. Cradling her newborn son, Brunhild lay among her pillows, covered with silk sheets and soft woolen blankets woven in the south of Francia. Snuggled against her, little Ingund, named for Sigibert's mother, placed a wet kiss on the baby's cheek, and Brunhild hugged her close. Even if she were only a girl, Ingund was her first child, and precious, with her rosebud mouth and soft yellow curls.

"It's good to see you smile again, beloved," Sigibert said, bending to kiss her brow and then the baby's.

"Partly, I smile because we have a son," she replied, "and partly because I'm told that Guntram's armies are ready to support ours. Chilperic shakes in his boots and fears assassination by his own sons. Merovech, the youngest, came to tell me so. He is our man, not his father's."

"That dainty sapling?" Sigibert laughed until tears came to his eyes. "He'd tell you anything you wanted to hear, Brunhild. Like all the young nobles, he's in love with my beautiful queen. The poor fellow turns pale and looks likely to faint when he sees you."

"Not all the nobles love me," Brunhild said, wincing as the baby's mouth pulled too hard on her breast. "Your Duke Rauching hates my influence over you. I hear stories about his burning his servants' legs with torches, then laughing when they scream. I wish you could get rid of him."

Sigibert sobered. "He's the richest of my Austrasian chieftains and the most battle-hardened. If we're to fight Chilperic and win, I'll need him and the other nobles he gathers around him."

"Once we've killed Chilperic," Brunhild said, "will you promise me that Rauching will be punished for his cruelties? We can't build Roman law in a country that tolerates a butcher like him. Men like Duke Gundovald are more to my liking."

"We can't control the nobles without Rauching." Sigibert strode to the door, ending the conversation. "I'll remember your concern, beloved, and see what can be done, once Guntram and I finish with our brother and his wife."

"Wife?" Brunhild sat up so fast that the baby lost the nipple and began to cry. "Fredegund is his wife?"

"Merovech told me she's now his father's queen," Sigibert said. "I'd thought to keep the news from you until the child was born. Your young swain is desperate for fear Fredegund will kill him off, lest he take the throne from her own infant son. He thinks that he should move against his father sooner rather than later."

"And we with him, husband," Brunhild said. "Merovech and Guntram and you can be allies, once Chilperic is dead. And they'll support our son, should we die before he is of age to take his throne."

"Ah, beloved, let us not think these melancholy thoughts, when we're graced with such children, such health, such love. Our little Childebert will need no one but us to raise him."

"So he's to be called Childebert? Your great-uncle's name? I had thought to call him Athanagild, after my father."

"He must bear a Meroving name if he is to lead our chieftains," Sigibert said firmly.

Brunhild bowed her head over the child. *What does his name matter, as long as he is to be king someday?* "We'll raise him as a Roman, though he's a Meroving," she said. "He'll be Childebert Augustus and will civilize his people. He'll teach them Roman law and customs."

"And not to wear bear grease in their hair," Sigibert teased, "or murder their relatives."

He left the room with a wave to her, and Brunhild lay back, the future king of Austrasia, and maybe of all Francia, burping noisily on her shoulder. Sigibert must have been thinking about how his father Chlothar had burned down the house of his rebellious son Chramn, with Chramn and his four children inside. No wonder the saintly Radegund had run away from Chlothar. If Brunhild had her way, once Chilperic and Fredegund had been dispatched, the Merovings would finally live together in peace. *I will marry off little Childebert as soon as he is old enough to breed,* she planned, *and give my grandsons Roman tutors. The Austrasian nobles will have nothing to say about how their next king is raised. I'll keep them at a distance. Men like Duke Rauching would try poison my son's mind, if not his dinner.* While the sun went down and the queen sank into sleep with her children beside her, she planned the future as if she were God himself.

Not long afterward, Guntram agreed, at Radegund's request, to parley with Chilperic, who was once again threatening to seize Poitiers and Tours. Venantius Fortunatus was kept busy, hurrying from Metz to Soissons to

Poitiers, trying to keep the kings from going to war. Back and forth negotiations went. First, Guntram said Brunhild must be given her sister's dower cities. Chilperic seemed to agree, then over the next few years, went back on his word, as Gregory had known he would. Chilperic and Fredegund now had two infant sons. Brunhild had given birth to yet another girl, so the Austrasian succession was by no means stable.

Chilperic clearly thought he was in the best position to win the favor of all the Frankish chieftains. Nothing mattered more to them than a strong king heading a strong dynasty, bringing the kingdom unity and good fortune. Though they professed to be Christian with their lips, Fortunatus said to Sigibert and Brunhild, the nobles of the north were pagan in their hearts. Whatever brought them prosperity was God's will, regardless of the lands they looted and the oaths they broke. Brunhild did not answer, since her own philosophy was much the same. The God-talk of Radegund and Gregory was all very well, but these holy people had no understanding of the world. It was past time to avenge her dead sister and destroy Chilperic and Fredegund. Brunhild would wait no longer.

She confronted her husband as he broke bread with Duke Rauching, perhaps not the best moment to choose, she realized afterwards. The two men sat at the laden board, eating, drinking, and laughing at war stories. When Sigibert was with his chieftains, Brunhild knew, he slipped back into the ways of his father and grandfather, drinking heavily and eating so much that he was sick on the floor. Someone had definitely been sick, Brunhild noticed, wrinkling her nose at the smell from the rushes under the table. Dogs hunted amidst the litter for bits and pieces of the dinner, not caring who had first digested it. Sigibert smiled at her hazily and waved his goblet.

"Come, my dear, drink with us," he said. "We're deciding the fate of the world."

"I fear for the world, then," Brunhild said, sitting down, but taking nothing to drink. "Is it finally time to fight Chilperic? I've waited nine long years for my vengeance. It's enough, husband."

Duke Rauching belched and poured himself more to drink. "You're not the one who'll stand in the front lines, Lady," he sneered at her. "We men will decide where and when we go to war."

Brunhild ignored him. "Sigibert," she said. "Husband, trust me. It's time. Young Merovech tells me that his father is losing the nobles' support because of Fredegund's atrocities. She murders as she pleases, cutting off hands and feet, leaving priests and nobles alike to bleed to death. If we can make Merovech king in Chilperic's place, we can control him and all of Neustria."

For once, Duke Rauching agreed with her. "I've just heard from my personal courier that King Chilperic got what he deserved for sending his son Theudebert to burn and loot all over Touraine. Our brave generals have killed the son and trapped the father at Tournai with what is left of his troops. Never was there a better moment to attack."

"And what of Fredegund?" Brunhild leaned forward, her eyes glittering. "Where is she?"

Rauching did not turn to address her, but spoke only to Sigibert. "Fredegund and her children are in Tournai with Chilperic. She's just given birth to another son, and so is too occupied to advise her husband. His troops and ours are massing on the Vitry plain, just outside Tournai. May I tell Duke Gundovald to proceed, my lord?"

"Let him wait only for us," Sigibert said, handing another drinking horn to Rauching. "You'll attack Vitry from the north, and I'll approach from the south. Chilperic will be cut off from his forces, and Merovech can take them for his own."

"King Guntram will need to bring his armies from the south to join yours," Rauching said, draining the ivory horn. "Or will he lie back on his couch and eat? I see no reason to trust him."

Sigibert frowned. "My brother has sworn to support me in this battle," he said. "True, he hangs behind in Burgundy, but he sends his troops to aid us. You're both right. It's time to bring Chilperic down. Merovech can be king in his place and will be glad enough of his new position that he will let me rule him."

Pursing her full lips, Brunhild looked a question at her husband, thinking that it was likely to be she who would rule Merovech.

But the queen said only, "At last we can bring all Francia again under one high king, as it should be." Brunhild breathed deeply and sat back in her chair. Her vengeance was at hand, she thought, and she would finally be at peace.

Sigibert stood up, taking his sword belt from a hook by the door. "Brunhild, you'll go with the children to Paris. It will be safer for you there behind its stone walls. I'll come for you when the battle is over."

"I'd rather be at your side, husband," she said. "Who knows what treachery Fredegund may have designed for you? If I'm there, you'll have eyes in the back of your head. I fear you'll need them."

When Sigibert did not reply at once, Duke Rauching stepped between the two.

"Madam, a woman is a bad omen in battle. In our legends, the only females on the field are the Valkyries, gathering the dead. If you intrude there, your husband will have his mind on protecting you, not on fighting. Go to Paris, madam, as he commands."

Sigibert nodded his agreement, and Brunhild thought it best to obey. A man about to fight an army should not have to begin by fighting his wife. Not wanting to distract her husband from his war, Brunhild bowed to both men, and went to her rooms to direct the packing of their treasure. Wherever she went, Sigibert's treasures would go with her—his queen, his gold, and his children. The least she could do was to guard these three.

Her husband came to visit her that night and the two talked and loved until dawn. Brunhild said good-by to him, sure in her heart that he would win this battle. God and the power of Burgundy added to their own Austrasian forces were on his side. Chilperic and Fredegund would soon be dead and her husband would be king of all northern and western Francia. Still, despite her confidence, Brunhild found it hard to let go of Sigibert, and took her time tying his armor on him. Because archers had become prominent in combat, even Roman commanders now wore chain mail copied from the Gauls.

Duke Gundovald, one of the most reliable of Sigibert's Austrasian nobles, arrived to accompany his king into battle. His scarred, craggy face was relaxed in a smile, reassuring Brunhild that the duke had no worries about the outcome of the battle. He had visited them the night before to say that Chilperic's forces were small and that his men were deserting him as the allied armies approached Tournai.

"It makes me nervous," Brunhild said to Sigibert and the duke, "that so many in our armies come from beyond the Rhine. They're savages, I hear, still practicing human sacrifice when the mood strikes them."

"Let's hope that Chilperic fears them too," Sigibert laughed, pulling out his sword and spitting on it for good luck. He no longer used the short Roman *gladius*, but the long *spatha*, a slashing weapon, particularly useful against unarmored cavalry.

"We know your brother Guntram does," Gundovald said soberly. "He told Chilperic that if the pagan hordes came into his territory, he would resist them and stand by Chilperic. A catastrophe for us, if Guntram does not bring his forces into the pincer, as promised."

"I sent a courier to Guntram on my wife's suggestion." Sigibert pulled on his helmet and strapped its leather sidepieces under his chin. "I told him that if he doesn't let us cross the Seine in his territory, I'll turn on him with my whole army, pagan Rhinelanders and all. It would serve him well for cozying up to Chilperic behind my back."

"The courier returned to us at once," Brunhild said to Gundovald, smiling as she braided her golden-brown hair. "Guntram was sufficiently impressed that he let our armies cross over his bridge at Troyes. There he'll meet with Sigibert today and swear fealty to him."

Gundovald nodded and smiled back at her. "He knows that if our soldiers from beyond the Rhine invade Burgundy, they'll turn it to burning cinders. I myself am terrified of these fellows. They'd as soon hurl a battleaxe in your teeth as parley."

"So you see, beloved, we're bound to win," Sigibert said, bending to give her a quick kiss. "Chilperic's been retreating steadily. He won't name a day of battle, though I've challenged him to it three times. No Frank has ever refused to name a day of battle, but my brother has the honor of a wild pig."

"And if Chilperic wants to talk?" Brunhild tossed one long braid over her shoulder, and faced her husband. "You'll cut him down like the animal he is?"

"I would offer him single combat," said Sigibert, "saving many lives."

Gundovald scratched at his stubbly chin. "Your foot soldiers want battle," he argued. "If they get no battle, they get no booty, and might turn on you, my lord."

"Let them feed on Chilperic's cities," Sigibert said. "While my brother hides in Tournai, my troops are slashing through Neustria, taking what they want from Chilperic's lands."

"Already the Neustrian nobles have sent to us, saying they will follow Sigibert, if he'll call off his Rhineland dogs." Brunhild cinched an embroidered girdle around her waist, wishing it were as slender as it had been before she bore children.

"And so I have," Sigibert replied. "The Rhineland hordes have enough booty for now, and must content themselves with that. I've pledged the

Neustrian nobles to treat them well if I become their king, and they know I keep my word, unlike my brother."

"As long as we fight Chilperic to the death," Brunhild murmured in her husband's ear, not wanting Duke Gundovald to hear her giving orders to the king. "I won't complain. But Chilperic and his concubine must die. I don't care what Radegund and her milksop friends say about peace-making between brothers. If it's a question of peace or justice, I choose justice, and trust you will too."

Brunhild tried not to remember the letters she had received from Germanus, the saintly bishop of Paris and from Radegund. They had begged her to remember that fortune had a way of turning the hopes of men upside down. God looked kindly on peace-makers, they wrote, not on those who would kill their own family. Brunhild had thrown the letters aside, muttering that these holy folk had no understanding of statecraft and no right to interfere in the business of kings. Besides, they seemed to have forgotten that Brunhild's own family member, Galswinth, had been garroted in her bed by Chilperic and his wife. *Let Chilperic learn how family should be treated,* Brunhild thought. *I already know well how to avenge my own.*

Having gathered her baggage wagons full of treasure, and dressed in a blaze of gold and jewels, Brunhild entered Paris on horseback, holding young Childebert in front of her, while the Parisians dutifully bowed and waved. Sigibert had demanded that the city, which all the brothers had sworn to keep out of the conflict, open its gates to him and his family. Cowed by the reputation of his Rhineland warriors, the Parisians invited Brunhild and her procession to enter.

She was happy to hear reports of Sigibert's royal triumph as he passed through Neustrian territory to Tournai, where his brother cowered. Chilperic's nobles rode their horses alongside Sigibert's Austrasians, all of them shaking their spears in the air, joyfully shouting the name of Sigibert, king of all Francia, as his father Chlothar had been before him. As they travelled north, more Franks than Gallo-Romans lined the roads, for whole tribes of Franks dominated the region, filling in the under-populated, plague-devastated areas where Romans had once lived. They wanted a king who would unify and protect them, and believed Sigibert was their man. Sigibert thought so too. He was ready to fight for his kingship and longed to lay an entire kingdom at his lady's feet, along with the heads of her enemies. No matter that they were his brother and his sister-in-law, for were they not murderers and cowards? Sigibert raised his sword and directed his men onward toward Vitry, telling them that God was on his side and wanting to believe it.

Brunhild heard the news of the fight at Tournai as soon as Sigibert won, for Radegund had sent Fortunatus to report on the war. His instructions were to remember all the details so that Gregory could write them into the great *History of the Franks* and to bring his news to Brunhild in Paris. He was to ride at top speed, as soon as the battle was finished. Radegund's hope was that he could soften Brunhild's heart, so that she could forgive her enemies and not slay them.

Fortunatus found the queen in her chapel. She did not seem to be praying, for her breath came in short, shallow gasps, and her expression was fiercely focused not on the altar, but on the sword in front of her. This sword was Brunhild's own, for she was determined to defend herself and her children, if the nobles failed her. Fortunatus feared they would, as had fortune and God.

"My Queen, I have news from Tournai," he said. "Have I your leave to sit down with you?"

"Did my husband win?" Brunhild's voice was shrill, on edge.

"Yes, but. . ."

Brunhild held up her hand to stop him. "Tell me everything, just as it happened, poet."

Fortunatus obeyed, his eyes on the altar as he spoke, his usually mellow voice grating as he told the story. From the beginning, he said, the campaign had gone well. Duke Gundovald had pinned down King Chilperic's army on the plain at Vitry, from where Tournai had been supplied and defended. King Chilperic, coward that he was, had fled into Tournai to join his family, leaving his generals to fight in his place. They were deserting the Neustrian king faster than Sigibert's army could capture them.

The shields of Duke Rauching's men gleamed in the bright morning sun as the duke's troops came from the northwest, their leaders riding before them on the shaggy, large horses favored by the northern warriors. Sigibert's Rhineland soldiers, with their strange, tufted haircuts, followed Rauching, brandishing their harpoon-like spears, so feared by the southern Franks. Once the barb hooked into the body, it could not be removed without taking guts and muscle with it.

Accompanied by the bulk of the Neustrian army and by the troops Guntram had sent to him from Burgundy, King Sigibert advanced toward Vitry, watching with narrowed eyes the little town and the plain before it. Chilperic always had some trick planned, he told his nobles. Let no one but the armed soldiers come out of Vitry or Tournai, the king ordered, for he would guard against treachery. An army he could deal with, but a woman armed with poison or a priest with a hidden dagger, Sigibert knew, could bring him down. Although his army made Chilperic's look like a mere scouting expedition, Sigibert's face was grave, and his eyes had a haunted look as he spoke to Fortunatus, who rode a little behind him.

"Poet, you must sing this victory, for victory it will be," the king said, "But my heart is suddenly heavy as a millstone. Perhaps the Valkyries are shadowing me with my doom. In my people's legends, it's often that way."

"God and His angels are with you," Fortunatus replied, not as sure as he sounded. "You are God's man, my lord, and your cause is just."

"Ah, poet, sometimes I think God stands so far above our little mortal combats that he sees us the way we see ants. Have you ever seen an ant war, Fortunatus?"

The poet shook his head, not wanting to say that looking at such miserable creatures as ants, grubbing in their dirt piles, was not the way he liked to spend his time.

"As a boy," Sigibert continued, "I watched an army of red ants tear apart an army of black ones, carrying off their dead and wounded, for all the world as ruthless as us men. It took five hours for the reds to win the day and take possession of the burrows belonging to the dead blacks."

"Didn't you intervene to help the losers?" Fortunatus could not imagine where the king was going with this story of his.

"Does God intervene? I was God, in this instance, and I did nothing." Sigibert shrugged his broad, armored shoulders and looked north to the plain of Vitry, where his troops and Chilperic's were moving into battle position. "Perhaps God cares only for souls, not for causes, as men do."

"God cares for justice," Fortunatus insisted. "And your cause is just."

Sigibert's eyes closed for a moment, and his strong jaw sagged as if he were suddenly old. "Do you know what our own Germanus, the holy bishop, said to me when I left Paris?"

"No, my lord." Fortunatus thought Gregory would be eager to know what the bishop said, and so made a point of remembering it.

"He told me this. 'If you set out with the intention of sparing your brother's life, you will return alive and victorious. If you have any other plans in mind, you will die.'"

"I think Queen Radegund would have agreed with him." Fortunatus was uncomfortable, casting his eyes around the field for signs and portents. He saw a flash of lightning across the cloudless sky and wondered what Gregory would make of it in his history. A comet would have been more decisive as an omen, but lightning would have to do.

Sigibert's eyes opened wide at the lightning flash. "I must admit that my queen wants Chilperic dead for his murder of her sister. Like it or not, I'm pledged to carry out my brother's execution. Let all happen as it must." He dug his heels into his horse's sides and galloped off to lead his army.

The pincers of Sigibert's forces closed inexorably on Chilperic's desperate followers, cutting them down like hay at harvest. When most of the enemy was lying on the field, in a mess of blood and shattered bone, a group of citizens from Tournai came out unarmed, waving banners and cheering Sigibert. A few of them ran to Sigibert calling out his name.

His men lifted him on his shield, holding him high overhead, chanting, "Sigibert is our king, king of all Francia. Long may our king live and reign! Victory, victory! Sig, our king, our sun!" The men shouted and waved their swords in the air in the delirium of winning.

Fortunatus rode nearer, wondering why the handful of citizens from Tournai were being allowed to come so close to the king as he was enjoying his acclaim, raising both arms up toward the sun above him, for all the world like some long-ago chieftain of the Germanic forests, worshipping his ancient gods.

"No," cried Fortunatus, his strong bard's voice rising clearly above the guttural shouts of the soldiers. "No! Let no one near the king!"

But as his words rang out, two young men from Tournai rushed to Sigibert's side, as if they had some urgent matter to discuss with him. They claimed to be deserters. Later, Radegund's informants told him Fredegund had promised these two great riches for their families and given them intoxicating potions that drove them into witless frenzy. They were loyal to their queen, who had just delivered her new son, and were wild to defend her. The two men were carrying scramasaxes, daggers smeared with poison in their carved metal blades, and the points of these daggers plunged deep into the skin and bone under the arms of the victorious king. Sigibert cried a mighty cry and fell dead on the ground, the shield that bore him tipping like a cup being emptied. He was only forty years old, in the fourteenth year of his reign.

Fortunatus took one last look at his king's body, and weeping, turned his horse toward Paris and Brunhild. Behind him, Sigibert's army disintegrated and scattered, each group to its own home. Nothing remained on the plain of Vitry but Chilperic's army, which was already surging north, to take back the lands Chilperic had lost.

As he rode for Paris, Fortunatus felt no poem come to mind. When she heard the news, Brunhild would not want the kind of poems he could write. He would be lucky if she did not have him killed on the spot for being the unlucky messenger.

He sat in her presence, his head down, not wanting to see her as he told her what had happened at Vitry. The queen's face was red and pale by turns, her hands first clutching at her heart, then ripping the fabric of her dress open down the front.

"O God," she cried, "you are no God of mine if you so betrayed my Sigibert. He was pledged to serve you, pledged to bring order and virtue to this kingdom, and you let him die." Her face became hard as petrified stone, and Fortunatus started back from her, his arm in front of him, suddenly fearing her as if she were the devil himself.

"From this moment," Brunhild whispered, in a cracking voice that sounded like a death rattle, "I abjure this God I once served and give my heart and soul to vengeance against the murderers of my sister and my husband."

"My queen, do not damn yourself," Fortunatus begged her, daring even to touch her arm as it slashed the air in futile rage. "Here, I have a precious gift for you. I think King Sigibert would have wanted you to have it."

"What?" Brunhild turned, her garments flying around her. "What gift could possibly help when I've lost all that mattered to me in a single blow?"

"You have your children, majesty." Fortunatus fell to one knee. "You have the future and your son Childebert, who will be king after his father. What I give you is for him."

"Then give it." The queen's eyes were like blue marble, dead and hard.

Fortunatus pulled the ring of power off his finger and put it on hers. It fit next to her wedding ring, as if it had been made for her. "My ancient masters from Greece believed this ring carried power and wisdom. Whoever wears it must win in the end."

"Ah, how I wish you had given it to Sigibert," Brunhild said, her voice breaking, her eyes finally filling with tears.

"It would have done no good, Lady," Fortunatus said. "King Sigibert won, indeed, but he was overcome by the dark arts of Queen Fredegund. I believe it was she who sent the men with poisoned daggers. She, who destroyed your husband."

"I think so too, poet." Brunhild turned the ring on her finger. "I will see that woman dead, and I pray that this ring of yours will help me finish her."

When Fortunatus had left for Radegund's abbey, Brunhild stood for a while in the center of her room. *The treasure,* she thought. *The children. Where could we flee? To Guntram? Yes, Guntram would give us sanctuary and take Childebert as his heir. Childebert II, my son will be, and he will wear this ring of power.*

Her head spinning with plans, Brunhild called her women to her and began to throw her belongings into wooden boxes with strong metal latches. *Fredegund will not have my beautiful things, not that cat bitch.* Brunhild gave herself over to cursing Fredegund, avoiding any thought of her husband. If she allowed Sigibert's image into her mind even for a moment, she would have to admit it was her own lust for vengeance that had drawn her husband to his doom. Sigibert had wanted to parley, sparing Chilperic's life, and she had said no. *It was my most grievous fault,* some part of Brunhild said to her, *most grievous.* Galswinth's death had likewise come on the heels of her sister's fierce advice to challenge Fredegund. Such thoughts, Brunhild knew, must not stay in her head, lest she lose her strength and purpose.

Her plans to leave the city for Burgundy came to nothing, since Chilperic's army had surrounded Paris, awaiting the arrival of their master.

One of her few friends among the nobles, the Gallo-Roman Lupus, Duke of Champagne, joined her before the siege, to stand guard over her and her children. Lupus had been trained to rule in the old Roman way, with a strong central administration. His vigilant and unswerving rule had done him no good among the Austrasian nobility, who turned on the duke as soon as Sigibert was dead. They burned down his estates and ravaged his lands, driving him away from his city of Rheims and sentencing him to death.

Duke Rauching's men, for they were the ones who persecuted Lupus, were determined to finish once and for all any kind of central government. Lupus had fled to stay with Brunhild, who shared his political views. His alliance with her, he told the queen, might bring down the Austrasian warlords, who were savaging the whole country in the days just after Sigibert's death. He and Brunhild plotted over meals and sent letters to every possible supporter, trying to assemble an army that could stand against the warlords, but did not expect replies. Everyone seemed to think Brunhild's cause was lost with Sigibert's life, and Lupus's cause with it.

The two friends and conspirators were having lunch in the outdoor portico of her refurbished Roman villa near the city walls, when a troop of horsemen thundered through the gates. Glad that she had sent young Childebert upstairs for his nap, Brunhild called for her few armed retainers, and stood up. Lupus drew his sword and stepped in front of her.

"You're disturbing the peace of this place." Brunhild's voice was loud and commanding, as if she, not they, were in charge. "It is your queen who speaks to you, the mother of your new king. Who sent you?"

"Duke Rauching has ordered us to take Lupus, the Roman traitor, back to Metz for punishment." The burly fellow at the head of the little band leaped down from his horse.

"You've destroyed my lands," Lupus cried in a fury, swinging his sword at the oncoming soldiers. "You might as well take my life, too, if it comes to that."

Brunhild's retainers were no match for Rauching's soldiers, but they rushed to his side, shouting oaths and insults at the intruders. In a few moments, clouds of dust rose around them and the clang of metal on metal sounded like the work of some insane smith. The men screamed and swore, gasping for air each time they swung their swords. One hand over her pounding heart, Brunhild took in the scene, then decided she must stop the fight before the inevitable Frankish bloodlust took over. In that event, Rauching's men would probably surge into the villa and upstairs, where her son lay defenseless against them.

Drawing a deep breath to make her voice strong, she ran among the armed men, calling out to them and grabbing the bridles of their horses to pull them away from the conflict. "This man Lupus is innocent!" she cried. "If you harm him, a battle will begin that could bring down the whole country."

The leader sneered at her. "And who in this country supports you, lady? We reign here now, not you."

Brunhild thought fast. "Guntram of Burgundy is sending me an army at this moment. He and I will restore order to Austrasia, and men like you will find yourselves outlawed if you go on your rampages."

The leader leaped on his horse, then sat and looked down at Brunhild, clearly unsure whether or not to believe her. After a pause, he replied, "Woman, get back into your house. We have not come to harm you or the child, but to bring Lupus to Duke Rauching. If Guntram invades our lands, we will destroy him. As for you, move away, or we will crush you like ground meat under the hooves of our horses."

"I will not forget your faces or Rauching's crimes," Brunhild shouted, feeling helpless as a fox run down by dogs. "When I come back into my power, you will suffer for what you've done today." Brunhild's words sounded like tinkling cymbals, even to her, and she was not surprised when the soldiers laughed and turned their backs on her.

Lupus was seized from behind and thrown over the saddle of one riderless horse, as if he were a sack of grain. Knowing she could do no more, Brunhild fumed as she retreated to the door of her house. Being stripped of power felt even worse because she had had so much power before. Now, all she could do was make idle threats and suffer contempt from all who heard them. *One more supporter gone, and two of my retainers dead at the hands of Rauching's men.* Brunhild surveyed the bloody courtyard and the bodies that lay in the dust. *It is likely,* she thought, *that mine will soon be one of them.*

She was not ready for the next blow. Duke Gundovald stormed into her rooms demanding to take little Childebert with him. "My lady, King Chilperic is near Paris. Your son will be his next victim if I don't take the boy back to Metz."

"Then you must take him." Brunhild paused in her packing. "What of my husband's body? Did Chilperic dishonor it?"

"That, at least, he didn't do," Gundovald said, covering his eyes with one hand. If he shed tears, she could not see them. "Chilperic viewed Sigibert's body coldly, but declared his brother should be buried like a king. Sigibert was dressed in garments of linen, decorated with jewels, and buried at the village of Lambres, with all ceremony."

Gregory had sent her a letter saying that in a moment of divine vision, he had seen God's sword hanging above Chilperic's palace, a sign that Chilperic would not die a peaceful death. Brother could not kill brother without incurring the wrath of God, he wrote. Brunhild was not comforted by Gregory's vision, but waited for Chilperic, quietly raging in the fastness of her house near the walls. Her young son sat on her lap, and her tears darkened his long yellow hair, so like Sigibert's.

"It's time for you to go, my son," she whispered, holding him close to her heart. "I'll follow when I can. You must be brave, like your father."

"I don't want to be brave. Being brave means I'll die," said the child, rubbing his eyes red. He had understood when Brunhild told him his brave father was dead, having just the week before seen his puppy die in convulsions from eating poisoned food no doubt meant for the royal family. The word 'dead' had meaning for young Childebert, and he squirmed in his mother's arms, trying to get closer to her.

"You will be brave," Brunhild said sternly to him, "and you will live to avenge your father. Swear it."

The child put his hand on hers and swore vengeance, although this word rang hollowly in his head, meaning nothing.

Gundovald's serving man came into her rooms with a basket. "It's time, my lady. The duke waits under the walls for me to lower the young king down. Be sure that we will keep him safe."

"I'll go to the walls with you," Brunhild said, throwing a mantle around her shoulders and wrapping her son in it so that he became invisible, a part of her.

She knew the boy was marked for death if Chilperic and Fredegund got their hands on him. Only that knowledge could make her give him up. The child clung to her as she followed the duke's servant up the stone steps to the windswept top of the walls. Once he had Childebert safely in his arms, Gundovald would head straight to Metz, where her son would be with people who had much to gain from calling him king rather than Chilperic.

Sigibert and Brunhild had long planned that in the event of his death, she would rule with her son until he came of age. The nobles would want it otherwise, but Brunhild would put them down. *If I can escape death at Fredegund's hands, the Austrasian nobles must let me be their queen. Gundovald and Guntram will help me.* Brunhild did not think of praying for God's help, since God had let Sigibert die. *God is Fredegund's friend, not mine.* She gnawed at her pale lips in fury, imagining what she would do to the murderous queen, were Fredegund in her power. Perhaps she would hire Fredegund's own torturers to finish the woman. They would have been taught how to kill slowly, and she would pay them that much better, the longer Fredegund's death took.

Brunhild kissed her son good-by, wrapped him in her woolen mantle, and secured him in the basket with a leather thong. In his lap she placed a large skin-bag full of her finest jewels, worth more than all the gold in her wagons. When the servant hung over the walls, carefully playing out the rope that suspended the basket, Brunhild leaned beside him, her stomach cold against the stone wall, watching Gundovald below, illuminated by his torch, hoping that the man had not been suborned by Chilperic to deliver the young king and see him dead.

Her heart felt as if a snake had wrapped around it, constricting it until it could hardly beat. She could trust no one. Not Gundovald, certainly not God. She watched as the duke took the child and rode off into the darkening night. *Let Chilperic come, I am ready. If he kills me, my son will still be king.* But her heart would not be at peace until she heard that Childebert was safe in Metz, wearing the Meroving crown.

The next morning, as she sat brooding by the window, her daughters on her lap, Brunhild saw Chilperic and his troops approaching her villa. At least Fredegund was not with them. She had given birth during the siege of Tournai, and was doubtless rejoicing in her husband's victory over Sigibert and in her many sons who would someday line up for the Neustrian throne. *Perhaps the throne of all Francia, if the evil queen can contrive to kill little Childebert.* Brunhild ground her teeth, wishing she could, with a single breath, extinguish Fredegund and all her brood. She was still thinking bloody thoughts when Chilperic and his attendants came trooping into her rooms.

"You are no longer a queen, Brunhild," Chilperic said, not bothering to wipe his muddy boots before he trampled her fine, silk-embroidered carpet, brought from Spain. "I demand you surrender your son and daughters to me. I will become your son's regent."

"My son is far away with his father's nobles," Brunhild said, her voice low and hard. "My daughters, as you see, are here, helpless. I suppose you'll have no mercy on them and their innocence."

"On the contrary, lady," Chilperic replied, sitting down across from her, cool as if he had been invited. "I'm not threatened by women."

"Clearly not. Look what you allowed your concubine to do to my sister." Brunhild wanted him to squirm, but he did not.

"Galswinth died of a fever," Chilperic said. "Don't believe rumors."

"And I suppose I and my daughters will die of the same fever?" Brunhild laughed harshly, feeling bile rise in her throat.

"Not at all. They will be taken to the convent at Meaux, where the nuns will watch over them. You'll be sent to Rouen, where a suite of rooms awaits you for an indefinite stay."

"Both cities are yours to command," Brunhild said. "I suppose I'll find no friends there and probably a garroting, as my sister suffered at your hands. Or your woman's." The word 'wife' stuck in her throat, and she could not utter it.

"You'll be safe, lady, my word on it." Chilperic smiled his feral smile, so like Fredegund's. "I've won the day and your husband's treasure. I don't need to seal my victory with the blood of helpless women."

He spoke with such contempt that Brunhild sank back in her chair, unable to reply. She had lost everything overnight, she suddenly realized, even the respect due a queen. Nothing was left, not her freedom, not her children, not her gold. *Chilperic and Fredegund might as well kill me and feast on my flesh*, she thought, saying nothing out loud. *They might as well gnaw my bones like Rhineland savages.* She watched as Chilperic's men took her daughters away and then followed the women he had assigned to her. Rouen would be her place of exile, she thought. From there she would plot escape, plot a return to Metz to guard her son, and always, always, plot vengeance against Fredegund, author of her ruin.

Rouen was not as bad as she had feared. Apparently Radegund and Fortunatus had contacted Praetextatus, bishop of Rouen, to counsel Brunhild and plan an escape for her. As long as she was imprisoned at Rouen, Chilperic could kill her at any time, and no doubt would, if Fredegund demanded it. Brunhild knew that such an execution would be managed with exquisite pain to herself. Fredegund had a reputation for skill in such matters. Praetextatus, she thought, was a weak, womanish man, who could not be counted on, but he was Merovech's god-father. Perhaps, if he would not help her for her own sake, he would help her for Merovech's. The boy had loved her once and perhaps still did. She was not surprised that when the bishop came to call on her, Merovech was at his side. Behind him was his servant Gaïlen, who had accompanied the prince through all his misadventures. Brunhild beamed at them, as if they were her best friends. For all she knew, they were.

"Sit down, my lords," she said, gracefully waving at a chair beside her. "Prince Merovech. How pleasant to see you again. I thought your father had sent you with an army to seize Poitiers, yet here you are."

Merovech fell on one knee and kissed the hand she extended to him. "I came here instead, my lady. Surely you know on what errand."

"I can only hope, my lord." Brunhild cast her eyes down and let tears flow from them. It was not hard to bring on tears, since the day she had heard that Sigibert was dead. "You see before you a woman in need of friends. I would like you to be one of them."

"Be sure I will." Merovech gazed into her eyes and held her hand too tightly. "You are as dear to me as life. Praetextatus, tell her."

"My godson proposes that you should marry him, so the two of you can bring Neustria and Austrasia together. If he can take down Chilperic, the union of Francia can be accomplished." Bishop Praetextatus stood wringing his hands, his voice quavering. "It's a bold step, and we may all die for it."

"Why should I marry?" Brunhild got up and walked around the room, her silk skirts swishing against the floor. "I could be regent for my son, in effect queen of Austrasia."

"The Austrasian nobles under Duke Rauching have declared that he, not you, will be regent, and that you have no power over your son or them." Praetextatus looked at her sadly. "Surely, you need a strong man at your side."

Brunhild stared him down, then looked at Merovech, with a question in her eyes. The young man had won a few battles, she knew, but people said he was melancholic, nervous, not to be depended on. At least, he could be ruled by her, Brunhild thought. She would be warrior enough for them both. She wondered for a moment if she should give him the ring of power that Fortunatus had given her, but decided against it. *Let the prince prove himself first. I will keep the ring until it gives me back my kingdom.*

"Well, Prince Merovech, you have a bride and a queen," she said, glad to see the warmth in his eyes. "I could do no better than have such a man, such a prince, at my side. Praetextatus, will you dare marry us? We are nephew and aunt, you know."

"By church law, a man cannot marry his aunt, even an aunt by marriage." The bishop looked from one of them to the other, then closed his eyes. "Merovech is my godson. I'll do as he wishes."

"Then let us proceed," Brunhild said briskly. "We must make haste to Metz. Surely the nobles will respect a regent who arrives with a prospective king on her arm."

"I hope I am more to you than that," Merovech said, his voice uncertain. "To me, you are everything."

"Of course, of course," Brunhild's mind was already on her escape. "I will love you well, as I did Sigibert. Never fear, Merovech. We will be a happy pair, once we rule."

In her heart, she was not stirred by the young man's fervent words or warm looks. He was not Sigibert. He was nobody, except a possible avenue to queenship. She did not even pity him for what he might have to endure when his father Chilperic found out what the boy had done this day. If he could not win against Chilperic in battle, so much the worse for him.

A faraway voice from her past whispered, *Blessed are the merciful, for they shall obtain mercy.* The voice sounded like Galswinth's and the words like those her sister would have spoken, echoing the words of Christ. Brunhild hardened her heart and the voice died away. *For Chilperic there will be no mercy, nor for any of his family. To make him fall at the hands of his own son,* Brunhild reflected, *would give me great pleasure. And Fredegund's infants? Let them be killed before their mother's eyes.* She smiled, bowed to the two men and had them escorted from her room. They would be waiting for her in the church. She need bring no dowry, Merovech said, his eyes hot with longing, being in herself dowry enough.

After Praetextatus said the words over them in his small, dim Rouen cathedral, Brunhild gathered up the few jewels and trunks of clothing that remained to her after Chilperic had raided her treasure, and left for Metz. She did not want a wedding night, and put off her eager young husband. Soon they would be together, she told him, but first, he must fight and depose Chilperic. When he was king of Neustria in place of his father, he would share her bed and not before. So Prince Merovech was sent away with the handful of troops he had left. He was to confront Chilperic and take the Neustrian throne if he could. Brunhild watched him ride west, slumped over his horse, too disappointed to sit up straight.

Probably, she thought, *he won't be able to bring off a confrontation with Chilperic.* Her new husband had many of his father's weaknesses, but lacked Chilperic's one strength—the armies needed to win and hold Neustria. Their only hope was that the Neustrian nobility had had enough of Chilperic's incompetence and Fredegund's crimes. Brunhild sighed, as she left Rouen, wondering if she should have accompanied her new husband on his venture. He seemed so very young, it was hard to believe he had ever won a battle, or that he could be man enough to win her. Despite her doubts, Brunhild was glad to see that he had acted as though he were in charge. Speaking like a king, Merovech had told his soldiers to escort her to Metz, and on his authority, they did. It might, she thought, be the last order he was ever to give.

Once in Metz, Brunhild struck with a confidence that was for the most part bravado. While the Austrasian nobles were in council, gathered in the great hall of the royal palace, she entered into their midst, wearing her finest regalia, purple silk layered over a gold-embroidered white gown. Ignoring their murmurs, she stood by the throne on which small Childebert sat, his face bright with pleasure at his mother's arrival.

"King Sigibert gave me the role of regent for our son," she said. "I've come here to take it. Guntram has given me his support. I've asked Duke Gundovald to be my vice-regent, and he's agreed. This is what I have come to say to you."

"You are bold, lady," Duke Rauching said, standing up so that he would match her height, "for someone with no power in this realm. We have Sigibert's son and need nothing from you. Go back where you came from, or we'll pack you off to a nunnery of our choosing."

So they would, Brunhild feared, since convents were the usual dumping grounds for unwanted queens. She would find a convent about as suitable a home as an eagle would find a groundhog's burrow. Life in such a place would be a kind of death for a woman like her. *I'd have to spend my time reading prayers, sewing altar cloths, and doing other little nunnish things that would make me crazy.* Brunhild knew she would have to show these men that if she did not have power now, she might well have it in the future. Rauching's pale malevolent eyes bored into hers from across the hall, and Brunhild steeled herself not to be the first to look away.

"I have married Merovech, son of King Chilperic, and heir to his throne," Brunhild declared, putting all her cards on the table in hopes of cutting Duke Rauching's support out from under him.

"Once he deposes his father, he and I will rule all Neustria and Austrasia. We will serve as regents for my son and raise him as a strong king, not one who can be pulled this way and that by whatever warlord has control over him at the moment. Surely, you can all see that Austrasia would be better served by a king who is unthreatened by Neustria and allied with Burgundy. Peace is to everyone's advantage, and peace is what I offer."

The warlords murmured among themselves, some moving toward Duke Gundovald, appearing to side with him and Brunhild. But Rauching stood his ground, idly toying with the hilt of his sword as he spoke.

"You are not aware, lady, of your new husband's capture by Chilperic's army. The foolish man is holed up in St. Martin's church at Tours. He's been shorn, tonsured as a priest, and is no longer a Meroving."

"I heard about this outrage," Brunhild lied, by a great effort of will not allowing her face to redden with rage at the awful news. "But Merovech will survive. His hair will grow long again, as if the length of his hair should matter, and he will rise against his father. Bishop Gregory is my friend and will stand up to Chilperic. He would never allow the king to violate sanctuary."

One of the Austrasian nobles who had gone to stand by Gundovald added, "It is said that Merovech sought out a witch for advice. She assured him that her augurs declare Chilperic will die within the year and a long reign for Merovech will begin."

Not very likely, Brunhild said to herself, *but let these brutes believe what they will, as long as it serves my cause and my son's.*

Duke Gundovald held up his hand to silence the babble of voices in the room and spoke to all the assembly. "I have just learned that Merovech has escaped from sanctuary. The new bishop, Gregory, grew tired of the

Neustrians carousing in the cloisters of the church, drowning out hymns and prayers. So he sent the whole lot to us in Austrasia. It is an opportunity to rid ourselves of Chilperic and Fredegund once and for all."

One of the bishops who supported Duke Gundovald chimed in. "Merovech laid his treasure and his prayers on the altar of St. Martin, begging the saint to give him his freedom and his favor. He is a pious man, I think, and would be a better ruler than his father."

Brunhild considered Merovech's unreliable nature, by turns aggressive and timid. He had apparently been bold in the sanctuary of St. Martin's, no doubt telling all who would listen of his step-mother's crimes and his father's cruelty, but how would he behave as a king? It was slowly dawning on her that she might have made a serious mistake in marrying the young Meroving. *I have been too quick to act*, she thought. *My grief made me desperate, and now I look like a fool before my enemies. Why did I listen to that fond idiot, Praetextatus? He would have told me any lie if it would advance his precious godson's interests.* Brunhild stirred in her chair uncomfortably, wondering what Fredegund would do to the wretched Praetextatus, now that she and her minions had their hands on him. His episcopal rank would do him no good on the rack.

She did not want to think about the story she had heard just the day before, that Bishop Praetextatus had been forced by King Chilperic to give up the part of Brunhild's treasure he had been commissioned to keep for her and Merovech, cloth and jewels worth three thousand gold solidi. Brunhild admitted to herself that she felt worse about the treasure falling into Fredegund's greedy hands than about the fate of the bishop, who was at that moment being dragged down a Roman road into Paris. There he would be questioned by King Chilperic in the presence of as many bishops as the king could collect, among them Gregory, newly ordained bishop of Tours.

Fortunatus would be with Gregory, having been ordered to Paris by Brunhild as her informant. Soon enough she would know the fate of Praetextatus. *One more victim of your dream of power*, the gentle voice in her head whispered. *Peace, Galswinth, leave me alone. Am I not suffering for my pride even now?* She looked down at her silver-sandaled feet, not wanting to see the jeering faces of the Austrasian nobles.

Shouts and scuffling just outside the hall cut short the debate. Everyone turned toward the door as a small procession of men entered with a rattle of swords. They swaggered toward the central hearth as if they owned the place. Brunhild was shocked to see Merovech at their head, with his faithful servant Gaïlen beside him. The young prince's blond hair was cut to collar-length in the usual Frankish style, with a tonsure on top, a bald spot that marked him as a priest. Incongruously, he was in battle dress. His footgear was fastened by long leather cross-garters, and he wore a tight, short-sleeved tunic, barely reaching the knee. Over it fell a fur jerkin, belted at the hips. A long sword hung at Merovech's side in a scabbard decorated with gold dragons. He had on a travelling cloak with a hood, which he had obviously used to cover his shameful priest's haircut until he arrived at the great hall of Austrasia. He threw back the hood as he entered, exposing himself to the derision of the nobles, but clearly hoping his gesture would be seen as bold, not ridiculous. For once, Brunhild was shocked into wordlessness and turned to Duke Gundovald for help.

"Prince Merovech," Gundovald began, trying not to smile at the astonishing spectacle of a Meroving lord's body with the head of a Roman priest. "We welcome you, but are unsure of your intent. Surely, you've not already dispatched your father and taken the Neustrian throne?"

"Not yet," Merovech boasted, with a warm glance at his wife, who looked away in confusion. "I've come to claim my bride, Queen Brunhild, and the support of Austrasia in the fight against my father. You all know that my step-mother Fredegund is a monster who has killed even more men than she has sinned with. As for my father, he's a coward who relies on his wife to murder his enemies by poison. Until the day he can be deposed, I want to stay here in Metz, at your court, if you will have me."

Rauching's eyes widened with disbelief. "You think to settle down in our lands with your aunt, illegally married as you are, and let us fight your battles with Chilperic? It won't happen."

His supporters shouted their agreement and raised their swords in salute to Rauching. Brunhild knew she was beaten before she opened her mouth, but opened it anyway.

"Lords, Merovech is no threat to you and would help Austrasia as a hostage against King Chilperic. We have seen that the king does not want his son dead. Let us hold him here, against the day when we must fight Chilperic again, as we surely will."

Rauching overruled her. "You will not keep your lover to carouse with you in the king's house," he said, jerking his shaggy head at Brunhild. "Go on your way, Merovech. You can't linger in Metz sucking on our kingdom like a flea on a dog. Seek pardon of your father, if he'll have you."

He gestured at his armed soldiers guarding the door. "Give the prince and his men a day's food and follow them to the Neustrian border. Chilperic will be grateful that we have sent his priest-son back to him."

Brunhild's cheeks flamed and she ground her teeth until her jaw hurt. It was not that she cared so much about Merovech and his fate, but that she felt herself slipping into a bog of her own making. She should have married an Austrasian noble, or perhaps Guntram of Burgundy, anyone but this short-haired Meroving who was a hopeless dreamer. He might think he was going off to do battle with his father, but she knew he was going to his death. The poor fool had no chance against the iron rule of Chilperic, enforced by the murderous wiles of his queen. For Brunhild, Merovech was already dead, and she was once again a widow.

When Merovech had been removed from the hall, Rauching turned to Brunhild and looked as if he would like to kill her on the spot. "Now, lady, we must deal with you, before you disgrace Austrasia again." He turned his head slightly, beckoning the soldiers behind him. "Seize her and take her to. . ."

"Wait!" Suddenly little Childebert climbed down from his throne in the child's way, turning first on his stomach, then letting his feet down to the floor. He stood in front of the high, red-cushioned wooden seat and said in his clear, treble voice, "I'm not yet a man, but I'm your king. Don't forget that someday I *will* be a man. When I am, I'll do very bad things to anyone who is mean to my mother. I want her here, with me. Arrange her chambers near mine, Duke Rauching."

Brunhild would have fallen to the floor if she had not been holding onto Gundovald's arm. She little expected rescue from her child, since she had come to Metz to rescue him. Childebert was like his father, Brunhild thought, not mere prey to be swallowed by some predatory lord. The little fellow stood as tall as he could, looking scornfully at Duke Rauching, as if the man were a grub on a leaf. Young Childebert knew better than to say more, but only waited for his order to be obeyed. Brunhild let out her held breath in a long sigh of relief. If she had still believed in God, she would have thanked him, but as it was, she thanked her child and the ring of power, which seemed suddenly warm on her finger.

Murmuring a little among themselves, the assembled nobles finally nodded their assent. Rauching knew when he had lost, but he would not so easily surrender the regency.

"Madam, you are a woman and unfit to rule a king," he said. "We must have a tutor for him. A *nutritor* who will guide him."

The words came as easily to Brunhild as if she were an oracle. Her Childebert must be taught Roman ways, not be allowed to be turned into a greasy, unlettered barbarian. One name came to mind, the only one who could serve her purpose.

"Gogo, then," she said. "He is known to you all and was Sigibert's counsellor. If you don't want me as regent, then accept Gogo as my son's tutor." She looked at Childebert, willing him not to contest what she said. She knew she could rule the fussy little man and through him, her son. Since Gogo was already old, he would not be around long enough to interfere with her guidance of the boy. Childebert nodded, his yellow hair brushing his shoulders.

"Gogo it shall be, then," Rauching said. "He will report to me, and together he and I will train young Childebert until he is a man. You, madam, will keep to yourself. We need no help from women."

Brunhild smiled her acquiescence, knowing she had won her place at court. In time, Rauching would lose his, and she would rule beside her son. She turned the ring of power on her finger as she followed Childebert from the great hall. As soon as they were alone in his sleeping chamber, she tucked him into bed, kissing him on the forehead.

"You saved your mother today," she said. "Your father would be proud. Now, I have a gift for you, beloved."

The young king sat up against his silken pillows. "What is it mother? A honeycake?"

Brunhild took his right hand and slipped the ring of power over his plump middle finger. It fit snugly, as she had hoped. "Never take off this ring," she said, "or let anyone take it from you. It was made by ancient masters who swore that its wearer would rule the world." As she touched the ring, she felt a thrill shoot through her like lightning.

Childebert studied the diamond, bright in the candlelight. "I can see my face in the stone. It seems to sing to me of my future as a king," he said. "Be sure, mother, that I shall always wear this ring and that it will bring glory to us both."

When she heard what had become of Merovech, Brunhild was glad she had given the ring not to him but to her son. Her young husband, poor in friends, treasure, and common sense, had been ambushed in a farmhouse that he had thought was safe. He and his friends had strayed far into Neustrian territory, into the wilderness near the Atlantic coast. As ocean winds whipped at the house and tall pine trees bent and snapped from its force, Merovech and his servants awaited the soldiers he had been promised by his treacherous contacts at Chilperic's court.

Sometime later, Brunhild heard the rumor that Fredegund had sent to her stepson men who persuaded the prince that they wanted to make him king. Just when Merovech had settled into the farmhouse and thought his new troops were guarding the door, he began to fear betrayal. Hearing the doors being barred from the outside, he was sure of it. Merovech leaped to his feet, imagining the tortures he would have to endure if he were captured, and crying to his loyal aide Gaïlen, "We have one soul and one mind, brother. I'm at the mercy of my enemies and beg you to save me."

Anything, my lord," Gaïlen stammered. "You know I'd do anything to serve you."

"Then draw your knife and kill me. I dare not commit self-murder. Do it, Gaïlen, if you love me."

Gaïlen did as he was told and dealt the prince a mortal blow. His kindness was not well repaid. King Chilperic arrived, took prisoner all who were in the house, and dragged them off to his palace in Soissons. There Fredegund finished the business. Professing horror at Gaïlen's crime of murdering her stepson, she had his hands, feet, nose, and ears cut off. *The woman is nothing if not thorough,* Brunhild thought, shuddering when she heard the news.

Not long after, she received a letter from Venantius Fortunatus, written from Holy Cross abbey and reporting on the fate of Praetextatus. All but one of the bishops at the synod had feared Chilperic's vengeance too much to fight for the life of their fellow bishop. Praetextatus was terrified when he realized that some of the nobles he had tried to win over to Merovech's side by gifts had actually been in the pay of Fredegund. Losing what was left of his slight courage, he threw himself at the king's feet, confessing that he had wanted to place his young godson Merovech on the throne.

"Do you hear this?" Chilperic cried, delighted with his victory. "Now, you bishops, declare your sentence on the criminal."

The episcopal judges put their fingers to their lips, encouraging each other not in conscience but in discreet silence. Only Gregory and one lesser cleric stood up for the abject Praetextatus.

"If you holy priests of God do not defend your own, you'll deserve to suffer his fate," Gregory said. "Counsel the king to leave off his persecution and beware the wrath of God, who protects his friends and punishes his enemies."

Though the bishops wanted to sentence Praetextatus to death in order to please the king, Gregory shamed them into a verdict of exile. The bishop would be sent from his seat in Rouen to an island in the North Sea, there to minister to the fishermen and pirates who lived on its stony shores. For Gregory there would be another punishment, Fortunatus feared, but the axe had not fallen as yet. Once Fredegund declared someone her enemy, anybody who helped the unfortunate fellow was her enemy as well, to be harried and eventually killed. He signed Radegund's name at the end of his letter and his own in small letters under hers.

After brooding on the letter's contents for a little while, Brunhild tore it up and burned the pieces. Fredegund had her spies everywhere and no information was out of her reach. *At least Fortunatus will not suffer from my carelessness*, she thought, *as so many have suffered from my foolish pride.* As soon as this thought came to her, she shoved it to the back of her mind, not wanting to examine it. She was a queen, after all, and had done only what a queen must do to regain her power.

Merovech should have been a better soldier, and Praetextatus a wilier priest. Their ruin is their own fault. Brunhild whispered these words to herself many times, but she could not quite rid herself of the sense that she had brought them down, as surely she had ruined her sister and Sigibert. From the day she heard of Merovech's fate, Brunhild took to praying for his soul's peace, though hardly believing in the God she prayed to. Her heart remained hard, but still she prayed, and at night slept uneasily, dreaming of Merovech falling at her feet, his eyes full of trust and love. *My fault,* Brunhild murmured, walking around her sumptuous chamber like a caged lion, *my most grievous fault. Forgive, forgive.* Someday she would have to ask Radegund who it was she wanted to forgive her, because she had forgotten.

When Childebert was only thirteen, he fathered a son on one of his concubines, and Brunhild realized it was time to find him a wife. She and Sigibert had promised each other that their son would breed young, so that the succession would be guaranteed. Now it was time. She brought Childebert into her private rooms, where satin curtains and flowered carpets might make the boy forget he was a warrior. A young girl whose father was a duke, stood beside Brunhild. Childebert had seen her before and fantasized about her, even telling his mother that he wanted this girl in his bed. Her name was Faileuba, and she was a pretty blond fifteen-year-old, whose fair face was flushed with embarrassment. She knew what Brunhild wanted from her and what she could expect from young king Childebert. Her father had told her she was to make herself desirable to the king, and Faileuba understood what he meant. She had dressed in semi-transparent flowing garments and adorned her face with paint. Whatever was expected of her, she would do. Brunhild despised her.

Childebert's eyes lit up when he looked at Faileuba, and the girl tried not to notice that he was only a short, pimply boy. Whatever he was, he would be her master and the father of her children. Faileuba glanced at Queen Brunhild, wondering if the woman had been in love with her own husband. The queen's face was impassive, cold as rock. Faileuba smiled at the young king, knowing that she had no choice but to love him. She said yes, for there was nothing else to say.

Ten months later, a son, Theuderic, was born to the young couple. Brunhild immediately hired a wet nurse, took the child from his mother, and raised him herself. She had done the same with his older half-brother, Theudebert, son of young Childebert's concubine. If one boy should die, Brunhild planned, the other would be king. If both lived, one would be king of Austrasia and one of Burgundy. In either case, it would be Brunhild who ruled.

She brought both of them to the baptismal font at the Metz Cathedral and took the role of godmother. After that, she cared little whether they were Christian or pagan, but bent them to their letters and to skills that would serve them on the battlefield. She meant them to be extensions of herself, as was their father, Childebert. Sometimes she would hold them up to a polished bronze mirror, telling them that they were gods who would someday wear the ring of power that their father wore now. They promised her they would fight against the sons of Fredegund and win, a vow she often reminded them of as they grew.

When they had run off to play their war games in the courtyard, Brunhild often sat in front of the bronze mirror and gazed into it, imagining Sigibert at her side, older now, but still beautiful. *That is the gift of early death,* Brunhild said to herself. *One never grows old, never loses the joy and power of youth, as I have.* Sometimes she thought of Fortunatus's song at their wedding, but only the words came back to her. As always, music was lost on her ears and even on her memory. She did not cry anymore and never exploded in fury as she had when young. But a heavy, silent sorrow lay on her like a gravestone. She mourned without ceasing, and if there were music in the air, she could not hear it.

*A new commandment I give to you,
that you love one another, as I have loved you.*
John 13:34
*Blessed are the peacemakers, for they
shall be called the children of God.*
Matthew 5:9

Book III

The Saint

Queen Radegund

531 A.D.

When she was only a child, Princess Radegund's uncle made the mistake of breaking a treaty with the Franks. The treaty had called for Frankish help in conquering his brother's lands. After the brother had been disposed of, Uncle Hermanfred was supposed to give half his lands to his Frankish friends. Hermanfred thought better of his bargain, once the old king and his wife were safely dead, and decided to keep the whole kingdom for himself. At least he had not harmed the old king's children, Radegund and her little brother, for Hermanfred was not as heartless or as thorough as the Merovings.

Three sons of Clovis came down on him like a force of nature. The Thorings, Radegund's people, had to defend their small territory, called Thuringia by the Romans, against the massed armies of Chlothar and his brothers, all as mad for conquest as their father had been. The realm of the

Thorings, still pagan and rural, proved easy pickings for the Franks. The simple Thorings did not know Roman battle strategies and still fought individually, man against man, in a contest that bore no resemblance to the clash of Romanized barbarian armies. The Thorings fought the Franks at the border, then fell back into their fields, and finally fled to surround the plain wooden manor house where their king lived with his family. There they made a last stand against their ruthless and well-armed enemy, and there they died almost to the last man.

Uncle Hermanfred had always been fond of his niece and nephew, who often visited his home in the days before he killed their parents. Princess Radegund and her little brother, Prince Berthar, had no idea what had happened to their father and mother, but assumed their parents would eventually return. They knew only that they now lived with their aunt and uncle and could play every day with their lively older cousin. All summer the children ran around the grounds of the new king's estate, until one day, their cousin and his mother disappeared. One of the servants whispered that they had been sent for safety to Constantinople because of the invasion, a word Radegund did not understand. She mourned the loss of her cousin, who had looked after the other two children, making them forget their missing parents. He had left his toys for her and Berthar. Though her little brother seemed content to have a new box of toys, Radegund could not be consoled. Only little Berthar remained to her, and she watched over him as tenderly as her cousin had guarded her.

Flowers were withering in her father's gardens from the early frost, and eight-year-old Princess Radegund hunted for the few living ones that were left. She had been told to go out and play with Berthar in the gardens, while their elders met to discuss the invasion. The little girl felt uneasy at hearing that mysterious word again, but trusted that all would be well. Her world had always been a gentle procession of seasons, with harvests, then snow, then rains, and finally summers, when the flowers spread across the meadows.

Radegund loved flowers and often sat on the ground staring into the heart of blossoms. Sometimes she seemed to fall into them like a dust mote, and nestle in their hearts, where all she could feel was their scent and their soft touch. The sound of bells tinkled in her ears, and she felt the flowers dance around her. But on this day, when she looked into the flowers, she saw only dead, brown sticks and heard them clatter together like dry bones.

"Radi, what is that noise?" Little Berthar stopped hunting for live flowers and stood up, his round face turned toward the sky.

"It's thunder, I think," the girl said. "Come, let us make a sacrifice to Thor. You know he is our special god. His hammer protects us." She hoped Thor would help his people in this time of invasion, whatever that was. He had not paid much attention when she asked him for favors like finding a missing basket or healing her sick mother. Still he was the god of the Thorings, all the god they had, and she would honor him with her prayers, as she did with the tiny golden hammer she wore around her neck as an amulet to ward off evil.

"Does Thor want dead flowers?" Berthar asked. "I wouldn't, if I were a god."

"We'll give him what we've found," Radegund decided. "It will have to do."

The two children piled their flowers on a stone, which Radegund said was like Thor's anvil. Berthar pounded it with his fist for good measure, looking as solemn as Thor himself.

"Great Thor," Radegund prayed, as a louder crash was heard not far from where they stood. "Care for us in our need. I do not know what an invasion is, but I ask you not to let it harm our people. See, we honor you with what is left of the summer flowers. May your great hammer strike wherever there is evil."

She felt more should be said to convince Thor that he should pay attention to his friends, but lacked the words. When Thor's priests spoke, it was always in formulas that made no sense to her. An obscure desire possessed her to pray from the heart with words that would go straight to the heart of God, but such words had never been taught to the Thorings. No sooner had she finished her prayer, when the hooves of horses shook the ground nearby, and a troop of men rode into the garden, trampling what flowers were left.

"No soldiers here," one of the riders shouted over his shoulder. He wore a gold circlet on his brow and his hair flowed down his back, as she had never seen a man's do. "Only children. Who are you, girl?"

Radegund stood as tall as she could and stated her name, adding that she was a princess of the royal family. Her brother stood close behind her, his face buried in her back. He was shaking, and she could feel that he had wet himself.

"What do you say, men, should we cut these royals down?" The long-haired king waved his long sword, laughing.

"I say we take them prisoner. They would make pretty little slaves." One of his men jumped down from his horse and took Radegund under one arm, Berthar under the other. "Or maybe hostages to assure the Thorings' good behavior."

"Tie them to your horse, then," said the man with the crown. "We'll see what my brother Chlothar decides to do with them. Mind they don't get in the way of the fighting."

So the two children were dragged along as the soldiers rode right into the timbered hall, with its high smoky ceiling. King Hermanfred stood in front of his throne, swinging his battle axe, as if in practice. He fixed the crowned, long-haired man with a glare and spat on the floor in front of him.

"You will leave my house," Hermanfred shouted. Then he saw Radegund and her little brother staggering into the room, tied behind a horse, and his voice shook. "Gods, you have the children! Have you no pity for the innocent?"

Hermanfred rushed at the crowned man, and swung his axe high. Not high enough or hard enough, for the other man plunged his long sword straight into Hermanfred's chest as if spearing a piece of meat. Radegund screamed as she saw blood and foam gush from her uncle's mouth. Pulling at the rope that held her, she strained to reach him. His blood pooled on the rough floor planks. Radegund could not cry out. Her throat seemed to close as if she were drowning, and her breath stopped for a moment. A dark haze shifted like smoke before her eyes, and she felt something deep inside her die as surely as if the crowned man had stabbed her, too. Reeling against her brother, whose sturdy little form kept her upright, Radegund gave up her small faith. *I will pray to Thor no longer, for he is dead to me and to my people. If there is some truer god, let me find him, or let me die.* She pulled the gold hammer from around her neck and tossed it on the floor. One of the Frankish soldiers pounced on it.

The body of her uncle was burned on a hastily thrown together pile of sticks that night, while she and little Berthar huddled together, watching what was left of their family dissolve into ash and blow away in the night wind. Nearby, several long-haired kings, one wearing a golden crown, threw marked bones on the ground as he gambled for ownership of the two small slaves. Finally, the tallest man won. He stood up, stretched his thick, fur-clad body, and shook back his yellow locks over his shoulders. One eye was closed by a purple scar that stretched from his forehead to the corner of his mouth, drawing it up in a ghastly half-smile.

"Stand tall, girl," he said jerking her by the chin and looking into her face with his one functioning eye. "God, you are a pretty little thing."

Radegund turned her head away. "And you are ugly as Loki, the evil one," she said, her voice so strong she was surprised. *Well, let him kill me for my honesty,* she thought. *He will do it anyway, sooner or later.*

Chlothar, for it was he, king of the Franks, laughed and gathered a handful of her honey-colored hair in one huge, filthy hand. "I will take this one for a wife someday and break her spirit." he said. "Send her to my royal house at Athiès," he said to the crowned man who had killed Radegund's uncle. "She must be taught all the graces of a Roman woman. I'm sick of these German wives of mine. They do nothing but spin thread and ride to the hunt. See to it, brother."

Not allowed even to say good-by to little Berthar, who was hustled off to some other royal house as a hostage, Radegund found herself wrapped in a stinking, half-tanned fur, and tossed over a saddle, her hands and feet tied so that she could hardly move. To her shame, she had to soil herself as she rode, for the brother of Chlothar would not bother to stop on his errand. Finally, they arrived at Chlothar's estate, a hall much grander than her father's. The lintel was carved with lettering she could not read and a freshly laid mat of rushes was on the floor. The king's brother rolled her off the horse onto the ground and called for the women of the house to clean her up.

Taking deep breaths so that she would not weep with fury and embarrassment at her filthiness, Radegund let herself be led into the house that would shelter her for the rest of her childhood. The Roman floor tiles under her bare feet felt cold, and she shivered. On the walls were shining stone pictures of solemn faces and here and there, a cross. She knew the figure, but not its meaning. Although she did not understand the pictures made of tiny stones, the faces seemed friendly, not what she had expected in this house of enemies. A woman with gray hair and a motherly smile led her into a room warmed with steam and gently stripped away her clothes.

"There, now, sweetheart, you will be clean and fresh like the flower you are." The woman, whose name was Gertrudis, lifted Radegund into the pool, where the child stood up to her chin in warm water.

"What is this called?" Radegund asked, breathing in the steam, her limbs loosening in the warmth of the Roman bath.

"Why, it's called washing," the woman smiled, perhaps at the little girl's odd pronunciation of the Latin words. "It's called a bath. You will come to love it as you love sleeping under furs on a cold night. Come, child, hold out your hands. I will give you a bit of ash to clean yourself and a soft rag."

The woman's voice was so kind that Radegund began to cry, not sure why the tears streamed down her cheeks, but sensing that there was still some good in a world that had suddenly turned as rotten as fruit in winter. She held out her hands and received what was offered.

Gertrudis, by actions more than words, taught the little princess to love the Lord Christ. Over their meals, the woman said a prayer in Latin that Radegund learned by heart, even before she knew its meaning. The words "Pater Noster," Our Father, touched her soul, and brought her own lost father close. When she said the prayer with Gertrudis and Leubovera, the woman's young daughter, Radegund felt herself open like a blossom eating light. Sometimes at church services she cried a little because she overflowed with music too rich to sing, too wildly beautiful to tame with notes or words. Leubovera would cry too, imitating Radegund as she did in all things except love of learning.

Together, they washed and fed poor beggar children who came to the door. Radegund's favorite game was playing that she was a priest and Leubovera her acolyte. First, she would polish the floor and the little table that served as an altar. Samuel, a young clerk, carried a wooden cross, and behind him, the girls led the other children in make-believe church services, using scraps of cloth for linens and borrowed kitchen cups and plates for sacred vessels. Radegund preached on the love of God, gathering her open-mouthed little flock around her to tell them stories of the martyrs who loved God so much that they gave up their lives. All the children had to promise her that they, too, would give their lives to God, and she presented each of them with little crosses made out of pine branches strewn around the estate.

Early in her stay at the Athiès household, Radegund mastered reading, first in Latin, then in Greek. As tutor, she had a young Frank named Gogo, who had studied in Rome as a child and had soaked up languages and literature as an infant nurses, with a frantic passion. He was a strange little fellow, she thought when she first met him, with his short hair and thin body, not at all like the warrior Franks who had brought her to Athiès. Gogo had a high voice and could sing beautifully as the songbirds that fluttered outside the open windows of the school room, the *scola,* as Gogo called it.

Sometimes Gogo sang Latin verses from poets whose works he had memorized in childhood. Radegund liked it best when he sang the *Eclogues* of Virgil, which transported her into fields full of flowers. There the sun walked on long, shining rays, and the sky showered rain like the happy tears of God, happy as her own tears in church. The words created music in her mind that sang her soul's longing for God. She heard unearthly sounds that felt like angels singing and stars dancing circles around the earth.

Gogo taught her to sing with him, and that was how she learned the Roman poets by heart, as he had. Her voice was so rich and sweet that Gertrudis said it was like the music of heaven's angels. When Gogo realized how well she could sing, he brought in a harp master, and had her taught to play the Greek harp. She learned the complex Greek scales that made gooseflesh rise on the arms of Gertrudis and Leubovera, who sang worse than frogs. Though they could not follow where Radegund was being led, they went with her as far as they could.

Gertrudis found a nun at a nearby convent who taught Radegund to sing the great chants of St. Ambrose, and the young girl's prayer, music, and learning began to fuse into a single-hearted longing for God. She read the lives of the saints and prayed for martyrdom. She read the Holy Scriptures and wished for the peace of God that passed human understanding. Everywhere around her, she knew, a slaughter of innocents was going on, but in the love of God there was freedom from human cruelty. *"Pax Dei"* she would say to herself over and over, *"The peace of God."* Her heart was already in heaven, and she longed for her body to follow it there. *Soon, soon, you will be with me, my bride, my love, my child.* These words often arose in Radegund's mind as she prayed, and she knew they came from the Christ who had brought her back to life with the music of his love.

"Gogo," she asked her tutor one day, "I'm sixteen now. Can't I become a nun like the sister who teaches me the chants of St. Ambrose?"

The little man rearranged the folds of the Roman toga he insisted on wearing, despite the cold weather. Real Romans, he declared, would never wear coarse *braccae*, the trousers of the northern tribes. "Princess, you are meant for another kind of life," he said, not looking directly at her as he usually did.

"But God is calling me to live only for him." Radegund laid her harp aside and leaned forward, her long blond hair falling like a veil on either side of her face.

"That you can do wherever you are placed." Gogo began to put away his books, signaling an end to instruction for that day. "Your learning will make you a wise and great queen. It is your destiny."

"But my kingdom has been destroyed," Radegund said, confused by his words. "I'll never be a queen." She had a moment's flash of her uncle's bloody body falling in front of a throne, so many years ago, his crown rolling away on the floor like a child's toy. "I don't want to be one."

Gogo stood up and put his hand on the girl's shoulder. "My dear, no one has told you, I think, that you're to be the wife of King Chlothar. I'm sorry to be the one to say it, but it's time you knew."

"Chlothar?" Radegund felt the blood drain from her face and sat down hard on the little Roman folding seat Gogo had given her for lessons in the *scola*. "That monster who murdered my uncle? Gogo, I'll run away. You have to help me."

He shook his head so hard that his short curls bounced. "Not I, princess. Chlothar would have my brains for breakfast. You'd need a braver servant than me. Accept the role God has given you and be a blessing to the

Frankish people. God knows they need one, given the treatment they get from their kings."

He looked around, suddenly frightened that his words might have been overheard. Then he made the sign of the cross. "We'll speak no more of your escape, if you care for my life."

So Radegund broached the subject only with Gertrudis and Leubovera, over their simple meal of bread, cheese, and wild dandelion leaves fried in bacon fat. "Is it true I am to be the king's wife? I need to know so that I can prepare myself," she said in calm, measured tones, as if the words did not sound to her like a death sentence.

Gertrudis dropped her bread on the floor, where a large black dog grabbed it before it could be retrieved. "I had thought to tell you later, dear one, when the time is closer. But yes, it's true that you're to be Chlothar's queen. The queen of all Francia."

"He has other wives," Radegund said, keeping her voice level, not letting her feelings show, even to these friends. "It would be against church law. It would be a sin that would damn both him and me."

"Nevertheless, you're bound to him," Gertrudis said, bowing her head as if she were going to pray. "God will not blame you for doing your duty."

This thought of damnation haunted Radegund from that day on, and she began to wear itchy shirts made of goat hair under her fine woolen tunics and to fast every day except for the light supper Gertrudis begged her to eat. In the middle of the night, when the itching woke her, Radegund fell on her knees by her straw pallet and said prayers for deliverance until she dropped to the floor in exhausted sleep.

Finally the day came when Chlothar called for her to be brought to him. They were to be married in Soissons, the capital of Neustria. When the courier came, Radegund gathered a few clothes, and without telling Gertrudis, left Athiès. She bound up her long hair under a shepherd's cap, wore a boy's clothes, and smeared dirt on her face, so that no one would recognize her. By sleeping behind bushes during the day, and running across fields by night, Radegund managed to get as far away as Poitiers, the place where God had told her she would find peace. She was barely able to trust even God, for whenever she trusted, she was disappointed. Now was no exception.

As she tried to enter through the city gates, Radegund was surrounded by armed men, who grabbed her cap, so that her hair fell down to her waist, and wrestled her arms behind her. She was Chlothar's prisoner once again, but this time she was no child. All the way back to Soissons, the soldiers taunted her with what she would endure when she became their king's bride. She heard every detail with mounting horror, and the soldiers laughed when she wept, mocking her with even uglier details about the wedding night to come. She was nothing but Chlothar's cow, they jeered, useless except to breed him sons.

Radegund's tears streaked the dirt on her cheeks as she rode astride a donkey, encircled by warhorses. She could not help but remember her Lord's journey to judgment and death when he rode into Jerusalem. *Lord Jesus, you are my God, my beloved, my only friend. I go in your footsteps. Help me to take up my cross and follow you.* After she had said this prayer many times, Radegund began to feel as if she were somewhere outside her body, where nothing and no one could touch her but God himself.

She was not brought back to Athiès, but directly to Soissons, where the wedding was to take place. Some women who were said to be concubines of King Chlothar, washed and dressed her for the event. They pulled her hair hard as they combed it, glad to inflict pain on the princess who had supplanted them. A large piece of polished bronze, a gift to the king from the Emperor in Constantinople, was placed against the wall, so Radegund could watch herself being dressed. She felt like a chicken being prepared for roasting on a spit, helpless and naked in the hands of people who cared nothing for her.

The king had ordered his idea of a wedding dress made, a crimson silk gown cinched tightly at the waist with a wide golden belt and a neckline cut so low she was ashamed that even women could see her in such revealing clothes. Men at the wedding would see the ugly dress and think evil things of her, as they had when they mocked her as being nothing but the king's cow.

After the women had finished with her, Radegund saw her tall, slim form decked out like the temptress of St. Anthony. Her large, deep-set gray eyes, with their long dark lashes, were bright with tears, and her small, delicate chin trembled as she looked at herself. *Beauty like this is a curse. It has brought me nothing but grief. Lord, deliver me from the hands of that brute who wants me. But not my will, only yours, be done.* Radegund turned away from her image and with an unsteady hand carved in air the sign of the cross.

The ceremony itself passed over Radegund like water over a drowning man's head. She knew many nobles had assembled around the cathedral, but to her ears, their shouts sounded far away and their insubstantial forms shifted before her eyes as if seen through dragonflies' wings. Chlothar greeted her at the door, and she gazed dumbly at him. He said to her later it was like having a corpse as a bride, her eyes were so blank.

The years had coarsened Chlothar's looks. His belly hung over his leather belt and his long yellow hair was streaked with gray. One thing remained the same, the purple scar that drew his blind eye closed and his mouth into a sneer. The king looked her up and down and wiped his thick lips with the back of his hand. Radegund held the edges of her low-necked dress together, trying to hide herself from his gaze.

"You are as I hoped you would be, a fit queen." He pushed her hand away and opened her dress down to the golden belt. "I would see more of you, lady, and will, tonight."

His men raised their swords, plunging them into the air, and shouted jests about the wedding night to come. Chlothar laughed with them, grabbed Radegund's arm and half-carried her into the church. The bishop, well-instructed by the king, did not ask if she consented to the marriage, but simply said the words that made her this man's possession for life.

Radegund kept her eyes on the wooden cross over the altar, looking at it so intently that the body of Christ seemed to appear on it. She forgot where she was in the intensity of this moment, for she felt her heart become one with the heart of Jesus, and she hung with him on his Cross. *Forgive them, for they know not what they do.* She heard the words she had read so often in Scripture, but this time they were said in a voice so tender and kind that she knew who was speaking to her. With Christ's love, she would forgive these strange, wild animals shouting around her as her husband dragged her down the aisle, away from the altar. With Christ's own love, she would love Chlothar, but not with a woman's love. Never that.

When the time came for the women to take off her clothes and put her in the marriage bed, Radegund was in a state of prayer so deep they thought she had gone to sleep. They prodded her to wake up when the king had come in, pulling off his tunic with no regard for the presence of the waiting-women. He sent them away and climbed into the bed with his young wife, who by the grace of God never even felt what he did to her. She was somewhere else, in a golden field where the sun walked on long, shining rays, and the tears of God rained down on her, washing away her own.

Early in the morning, Radegund woke up, not certain at first where she was. Chlothar's heavy snorts reminded her, and she looked over her bare shoulder at the naked stranger beside her. He lay on his back, mouth open, hair matted behind his head, smelling of ale and bear grease. Remembering her promise to love this man as Christ loved him, Radegund took a deep breath and tried to see him as a mother sees her child, an attempt that failed as fast as it was begun. *Well, I will try again when he doesn't look quite so gross.*

Radegund slipped out of bed and put on the woolen shift that had been left for her by the waiting-women. Kneeling on the cold floor, she realized that she hurt all over her body, as if someone had kicked her in every sensitive place. *So must the Lord have felt when he was beaten by the Roman soldiers, then made to carry his Holy Cross, much heavier than mine.* Radegund was thankful that

Christ had snatched her up, senseless, into his arms the night before, so that whatever Chlothar had done to her body had not been known by her soul.

When Chlothar called her name in his gruff voice, Radegund was so deep in prayer that she did not at first hear him. He hung over the side of the bed and stared down at her.

"So you find the stone floor more comfortable than my bed?"

"I must say my morning prayers, my lord." Radegund folded her hands and closed her eyes, wanting to blot out the flushed, scarred face.

"I've got me a nun," Chlothar grumbled, sliding back under the fur cover, "not a wife. Get up here, girl."

This time, Radegund could not escape knowing exactly how heavy her cross was going to be. She turned her face away from Chlothar's and tears slid from under her tightly closed eyelids. Her prayers went on behind her clenched teeth, and she made an effort to see herself once again in the sunny fields, gathering flowers that out of their scented mouths sang love songs to the God who made them. And so she drifted between dream and waking, letting Chlothar do to her whatever he wanted.

At last he seemed to be sated, for he sat up and said cheerfully to her, as if they had just been playing backgammon, "Well, my pretty lady, what would you like for a morning-gift? It is your right to name some gift for yourself, since I took away all your family's wealth."

Trying not to remember the bloody occasion he referred to, Radegund pulled the coverlet up to her chin and considered. *Lord Jesus, help me to find some gift that would redeem this man. Help me to love him as you do.* These words almost said themselves in her mind, she had prayed them so often. The Lord had told his people to ask and they would receive. Well then, she would ask.

"If I might have the villa at Athiès," she ventured in a soft voice, "I would like to make it a haven for women who have nowhere else to go. Gertrudis would be the one who cares for them. Could I have it as my own?"

"No jewels? No cities?" Chlothar shook his head. "Girl, you ask too little, considering your worth. I will give you the estate at Saïx and the city of Peronne, as well as the villa at Athiès. And enough treasure to do what you wish with these places."

Radegund bowed her head. "Thank you, my lord. I'll have prayers said there for your soul every day."

Laughing, Chlothar chucked her under the chin as if she were a cute puppy. "Well, I suppose prayers would do me no harm. Now, will you smile? I've never seen you smile."

Imagining that it was her Lord Jesus giving this command, not her brute of a husband, Radegund looked up at him and smiled so radiantly that Chlothar drew back, seeming uncertain what to make of her.

"I'd not thought to see such a thing, a sight like sunrise," he said, the words falling clumsily from his lips. "Lady, unless I take care, you might make a Christian of me."

He went lumbering off to the privy, carrying his clothes from the night before and muttering to himself about the strangeness of women.

Radegund curled up on her side, glad when Chlothar left the bed. She prayed as she went back to sleep, thanking God for blessed rest in a bed without Chlothar. The morning was long past by the time she got up and dressed, with the help of her waiting-women. *They treat me differently now*, she thought, *like their queen, but I don't understand what has changed.* Perhaps Chlothar had spoken to them, but it was unlikely that the man had given her a thought, once he was out of their bedroom.

When she was alone again, Radegund decided to explore the palace, hoping to find a chapel, a library, anywhere she could hide from Chlothar and his men. The palace was not so big that hiding would be easy. It spread out, rather than up, with rooms apparently added on by builders having no thought for art. A bedroom might be next to a chicken coop, or a kitchen next to a sheepfold. At least, someone had built an outhouse within an easy walk from the royal bedroom, and a bath house was built nearby as well. She put her head in the door and heard screaming.

"I'm drowning, you stinker," spluttered a small boy, fighting off a bigger one. "My mother will beat you if you drown me."

"And mine would beat *her*," the other boy sneered. He had long reddish-brown hair and small features, close together, leaving too much of his face blank.

For a moment Radegund's sight blurred, but when she wiped her eyes, there were no tears. A sudden picture flashed before her of these two boys grown to manhood and covered with blood. In her vision one cut down the other, but she could not tell which one was the killer.

"Stop it right now," Radegund called to them, stepping into the small, over-heated room. "I command you in the name of God to behave like Christians."

Both boys stood still, the water coming up to their mouths. The smaller one who had feared to be drowned had shoulder-length golden hair and a face that looked to Radegund like an angel's.

"What's your name, child?" She said, reaching down to touch his head in a blessing.

"I'm Sigibert, Lady. I think you're my father's new wife." The boy nodded his head respectfully, then coughed as he caught a mouthful of water pushed at him by his companion.

"Chilperic is my name," said the other boy, not waiting to be asked. He gave Sigibert a push and stood in front of him. "Chlothar's my father too. I'll be king of Neustria someday. My father says I will."

Radegund crouched down beside the pool and studied them thoughtfully. "And will you be intelligent kings?" she asked. "Do you know your letters?"

"A little," Sigibert said. "Only what our older brothers have taught us. They're warriors, though, not scholars. I'd like to know more."

"And so would I," Chilperic chimed in, determined to be noticed and valued. "But we have no teachers."

"Then I'll be your teacher," Radegund said. "Does this house have a room with books in it? A chapel? Anywhere that's quiet?"

"Our chapel is at the east end of the palace," Sigibert said. "We'll get dressed and meet you there. Have you any books?"

"I have the Holy Scriptures and the lives of many saints," Radegund assured him. "And I have papyrus to write on. We will make our own books."

The boys arrived at the chapel as Sigibert had promised. They were clean, damp, and eager to learn. Since Radegund had thought Sigibert would prove the more apt student, Chilperic's zeal surprised her, The wiry, tight-featured Chilperic learned his letters in a week and reading in a few weeks more. He loved Radegund's praise and said that someday he would marry a woman as beautiful as his teacher.

Sigibert, who was slower at his lessons, perhaps because he was younger and fidgeted too much, decided that he, too, would marry a beautiful princess from a faraway land when he was a man. Both of them declared they would marry Radegund herself, if she had not already been married to their father. They vied for her attention, learning at a rate impossible had they not been rivals.

By the time Radegund had been their tutor for half a year, Chlothar noticed that the boys were being guided in a way they had not been before. Sigibert had continued to excel at swordplay and spear-throwing, but Chilperic had ignored his war training to concentrate on books.

"Have you bewitched the boy?" Chlothar said to her over dinner one night. "He is clumsier on the practice field every day."

"I only want Chilperic to read and write like a Christian prince," Radegund replied, serving her husband more wine. She had noticed that he was less amorous the more wine he consumed at dinner.

"It's true he's only a third son," Chlothar said, subsiding into his cups. "And he will never make the warrior Sigibert will. That boy will be a king to be proud of. Teach them to read the battles of Caesar, wife. I want them to be warriors, not priests."

Radegund did as she was told, teaching the boys to read Caesar's *Gallic Wars* along with Holy Scripture. If they saw a conflict between the two, they did not speak of it.

As the years passed, young Chilperic insisted on writing verse and studying the Latin poets, determined to outshine his brother in learning. Radegund was kind to them both, as others had been kind to her when she was a child. She knew that these boys would have no example of kindness, except for hers. Their father treated them as if they were his serfs, not his sons, clouting them alongside the head when they were less than perfect on the practice field and ignoring them at all other times. She seldom saw them with their mothers, who were both ignorant women, caught up in their hope to produce another son with Chlothar. To them, what they wore and how their faces were made up were their only concerns. Their sons were Chlothar's to raise, and they gave the boys no thought.

Sometimes Radegund took Sigibert with her to visit the women's refuge at Athiès. Chilperic was bored with her charitable projects and elected to stay at home. Sigibert, however, took great interest in the management of the household. He followed Gertrudis and Radegund around the estate, asking questions.

"Why did these women and their children have nowhere to live?" he asked, pointing to the women working in the garden. "Where are their men?"

Radegund took his question as seriously as if he had been a grown man and a king already. "Their men are dead in war," she said. "I hope that when you're a ruler you'll keep the peace, so children can grow up with both their parents."

Sigibert nodded thoughtfully, walking along beside her with his hands clasped behind his back, as he had seen his father do. "Sometimes wars must happen," he said. "When I'm a king, I won't start wars, but end them."

"I know you will, my dear," Radegund said, touching his head lightly in an unspoken blessing. "And I will remind you, if you forget. Agreed?"

"Agreed." Sigibert gestured at the villa behind them. "And who made this place a refuge? Why?"

"Your father and I did." Radegund stopped by a crumbling stone bench and drew the boy down beside her. It was time, she thought, to teach him something more than Latin grammar.

"Because, my son, we who are rich in this world's goods must take care of those who are poor, as our Lord Jesus taught us. Our goods are not our own, but held in trust for the powerless."

"That's what it means to be a king?"

"That's what it means to be a Christian king," Radegund said. "We kings and queens are servants of the servants of God. We love our people as God loves us, like a Father."

"My father's not like that," Sigibert said, looking puzzled.

"No," Radegund sighed, "he's not. But God willing, you will be."

On their way home, they passed a pagan temple where the Franks had left the bodies of sacrificed animals and wreaths of flowers. The temple was not very big or very grand, and had open windows pointed at the top, where saplings had been tied together, like fingers pointing to the sun. Christian churches were built the same way, often on the same places that pagan temples had been. The roofs were nothing but branches lying on top of timber trusses, so that rain fell through and made the temple seem half human construct, half forest. Radegund got down from her horse and walked around the temple, making the sign of the Cross.

"The Lord Christ has said God wants mercy, not sacrifices," she told the soldiers who guarded her. "We must burn this place before any more animals are killed to honor false gods."

A crowd of Frankish pagans came near them and grumbled, shaking their farm implements at her like spears. "We don't want your Christ here," the leader said. "Our gods are strong, and they're all we need."

Radegund held up her hand for silence and got it. "I was once as you are," she said, "praying to Thor, the ancient god of my people. He did not answer, and my people died. The Lord Christ answers prayer and will love you if you turn to him. I must show you the truth. Watch and see if your pagan gods strike me down for what I do."

Taking a torch from one of her soldiers, Radegund hurled it into the temple and stood watching as the place burned. "You see, the old gods are dead, and our Christ lives. Live in his love, my people, and be free from the delusions of our ancestors."

The Franks muttered angrily, coming close to her as they swung their pitchforks and axes. "We're Odin's men and will kill you in his name for burning down his temple."

Sigibert got off his pony and stood beside Radegund, defying any of the Frankish pagans to attack.

"Listen to her," he said. "She's your queen and has told you the truth. I believe her and so does your king, my father. Now, pray to these false gods no longer and let us pass."

To Radegund's surprise, the Franks backed off and said no more. Sigibert had carried himself like a king, and she commended him for it. Later, when she sat with Chlothar over dinner, she praised his son again.

"I trust you're not making him into some kind of priest," the king said, pausing after he had speared a piece of meat. "I don't want the boy spoiled for kingship."

Radegund pushed her lentils around the wooden platter in front of her. "He's a wise young man. It's Chilperic who should concern you, husband, or so I think."

Shrugging, Chlothar spoke around the meat he chewed. "Chilperic's a fool, always scribbling and talking to women. Is that what you mean?"

"He's no Christian," Radegund said. "Already, despite his youth, he allows the servant girls to corrupt him."

Chlothar laughed. "I did the same as a boy," he said, "and fathered many Merovings. Let the boy make new warriors as soon as he can."

"I'm sure he will," Radegund sighed, "and they'll do the world as little good as Chilperic."

"Well, my pretty wife," Chlothar said, wiping his mouth with his hand, then catching her disapproving glance, used a bowl of water to wash his hands. "You'll have to do all the good for us, since we're such sinners."

"Then husband, I have a boon to ask of you." Radegund pushed her plate away, and leaned toward him, her light eyes fixed on his.

"Speak. I suppose you want more cities?"

"No, I want to spend some of the treasure you have given me on freeing captives. As you know, many of my Thoring people are still slaves among the Franks. I want to pay their masters to send the Thorings back where they came from. May I do that?"

Chlothar's face wrinkled in thought. "What if they rise in rebellion against my rule?"

"You have my brother Berthar and me as your hostages," Radegund said. "On our heads be it if our people do you wrong."

"I'll proclaim their freedom tomorrow, then," Chlothar promised. "Will that satisfy your Christian charity, wife?"

"I hope it will be seen as your charity, my lord. God will bless you for it."

Chlothar refused the wine she offered him, and came to her room that night, hoping for a more tangible reward than the grace of God. In the middle of the night, she begged his leave to visit the privy, and huddled there in the cold and stink, praying for deliverance. The privy felt like a cleaner place than Chlothar's bed.

Radegund got her answer a few weeks later. Sigibert, though still a boy, had gone off to his first war, against her people. They had risen against Chlothar as soon as they returned from slavery and exile, and he had promised to punish them. If the blood of her people was on his hands, Radegund swore on the relics of St. Médard that she kept by her bedside, those hands would never touch her again.

That night, Chlothar summoned her to an execution, but did not say whose it was. Her women murmured behind her back that someone's head would roll for the rebellion of the Thorings. Radegund hoped it would be hers, and was ready for whatever was God's will. She went to the great hall, dressed in a plain dark dress that covered her like a shroud. Her long hair was braided behind her back, and she folded her hands in prayer as she walked into the room. If she had to die for her people's freedom, so be it.

When she saw her brother Berthar, now a young man, well-built and handsome, kneeling on the floor, a swordsman lifting a weapon over Berthar's neck, Radegund cried out. "No, take me instead."

But the swordsman, at a nod from Chlothar, swept her brother's head from his shoulders. Radegund fell on her knees, unable to weep, even to pray. *How can I ever trust again? O God, you have thrown me into the pit of hell.* Her mind turned numb and her eyes darkened as if it were she who had been struck dead.

"Radegund, my queen, it was not my will to kill your brother," Chlothar said, jumping to his feet. "Your people rebelled and their hostage had to be killed. It is the way things happen in this world."

As someone lifted her and carried her from the room, Radegund murmured, "Then I must leave this world and you."

When she awoke in the middle of the night, tears still flowing from her eyes, Radegund gathered a few of her books, wrapped herself in her plainest cloak, and left the palace. Her favorite horse, a strong white mare named Glory, was led out by the stable boy, who knew her odd habits and thought nothing of this request to ride Glory in the middle of the night. Radegund rode alone to Noyon, and left Glory in the hands of the bishop's stable servants. Exhausted and aching from the long ride, she went into the church and lay prostrate before the altar. There Bishop Médard found her in the morning.

"My lady queen," he said, frightened and astonished. "What are you doing here? Where is the king?"

Radegund sat up, leaned against the altar, and rubbed her eyes. "I claim sanctuary. My husband the king has murdered my brother, and I will no longer live with him."

Médard, a skinny, gentle man sat down beside her on the floor, wiping away the sweat that gathered on his brow.

"You know the king will want you back," he said. "And he has the right to take you."

"Bishop, I know that and also that you are Chlothar's favorite. He'll do you no harm if you consecrate me as a deaconess. It's the will of God. That too, I know."

Médard scratched at his neckpiece, which felt suddenly too tight. "'Art thou bound unto a husband or wife? Seek not to be loosed.' So the Holy Scriptures say."

"I am bound to God only," Radegund replied. "As are you."

The bishop did not know how to answer her, but spread his hands helplessly.

"It is morning," Radegund told him, as she kneeled before the altar. "You will say Mass, and I will pray for us both, that we may be strong enough to serve God, not man."

The two were the only people in the small Noyon cathedral when Médard finished the service, and he looked anxiously at the door, wondering when soldiers would burst through, ready to claim the runaway queen. He had not long to wait.

Chlothar sent his soldiers to round up Radegund like a criminal. They came to Médard in his cathedral, as he read his afternoon office, and he stood to meet them on legs that trembled. Chlothar had always been good to him, but Médard feared that if he went against the king's will, the city of Noyon would suffer, as would he.

"The queen claims sanctuary here," he said, his voice sounding high and weak. "She must be granted it."

"Priest, we know nothing about such things," the officer in charge said. "I must take the queen back, for her husband desires her presence."

"It's not so simple." Médard gave him a letter for Chlothar. "The king must bow to church law in matters like these."

"The nobles of the realm support the king," the officer replied. "The queen is required. There is no more to say."

He grabbed Médard by the bishop's scrawny neck and pulled him down the central aisle of the cathedral. The bishop kicked and flailed, but could not free himself. At the door, the officer let him go, and Médard staggered against the stone pillar supporting the lintel.

"Take my letter to Chlothar," the bishop said, holding out the parchment missive he had written the night before. "I must speak to him before you take the queen from sanctuary."

Radegund had run from the altar and stood at the door, her hair swinging wildly around her pale face and her hand held toward the sky.

"You've done violence to a holy bishop," she cried out, her voice strong and rich with its singer's power. "God will strike you dead if you do it again. Leave this place, soldier, while you still can."

The officer started back, his eyes wide. "Very well, my queen, but I think you'd best stay here until I come back with the king's reply."

He took one last frightened look at Radegund, who stared him down. Then he shoved the folded letter into his belt and rode off.

For the time being, Radegund was safe, but she knew Médard wavered. Just to be sure she had the support she needed, she wrote a letter to the famous Bishop Germanus of Paris, the only cleric Chlothar respected. If Médard collapsed, Germanus would stand firm. She knew her man. *Germanus would go to the stake before he would betray his Lord,* Radegund said to herself, *or let a single one of the Lord's lambs be lost.*

The day after Chlothar's troops left Noyon, she came to the bishop, dressed in a dark gray woolen dress that fell from her neck to the floor. She had cut her hair short and thrown a veil over it, wrapping the thin gray fabric under her chin. Médard was just starting to say Mass when this monastic apparition, with a pale white face and tears falling steadily, stood at his altar.

"Bishop Médard, I ask you in the name of God, to consecrate me as a deaconess."

"My lady," he stammered, "you know I cannot. You're the wife of the king, my patron. I can do nothing more for you."

Radegund fixed him with her large, shining eyes. "Pastor, if you're afraid to consecrate me, if you fear man more than God, you'll see your lamb's soul snatched from your hands. What is Caesar's is Caesar's; what is God's is God's. These are the words of Our Lord, and we must hear them."

Médard gave in. "I'll do as you ask, Lady," he said, gathering the sacramental oils for the ceremony, "but you should go far away. My church cannot be your sanctuary."

Bowing her head, Radegund said, "Once I am ordained a deaconess, only God will be my sanctuary."

She received her ordination, and with two of Médard's retainers, she rode Glory far south to Saïx, an estate Chlothar had granted her when they were married. From the city, she would receive revenues that would allow her to serve the poor. From the estate, she would gain shelter and peace. No one but God would be her master.

The Pyrenees rose in the distance, white capped and glowing pink in the sunset, when Radegund rode Glory to the edge of the foothills above Saïx. She smelled the fields full of wild thyme and took in deep draughts of the mountain air blowing down on her from the faraway Pyrenees. They looked to her like a mother's breasts, full of sustenance and strength. Below her lay the little Roman town she owned and the people who would be her children. The villa looked small from such a height, but she knew it was well-equipped with a bath house, a guesthouse and a chapel.

She had already sent to various priestly friends for holy books to stock a library at the villa. Leubovera would be waiting for her there, having been told to make the villa ready for her mistress. Nothing remained but to write a letter to Chlothar asking that he free her from her marriage vows and to send that letter back with Médard's retainers.

Dismounting in the small courtyard of the villa, Radegund surveyed the place which seemed to welcome her with outspread arms. Two ends of the villa curved around the courtyard in an embrace that promised sanctuary. Radegund breathed a prayer of thanks and went directly to the chapel, which Leubovera had decorated with flowers and candles. Radegund prostrated herself on the polished stone floor in front of the altar and prayed until she fell asleep, unaware that Leubovera covered her with sheepskins in the night.

The newly ordained deaconess dreamed that she was riding Glory up into the mountains, then into the clouds, then through the gates of heaven. As she rode through the infinitely high gates, bright-shining with jewels, she lifted her arms to the tall, white-robed figure coming to greet her, his hands and forehead marked with the blood of redemption. He smiled and gathered her into his arms, like a shepherd with a lost lamb. Radegund whispered in her sleep, "My Lord," and he answered in words only she could understand.

Chlothar was not to be dismissed easily. He threatened first to send soldiers to take her home. When that tactic failed to produce his runaway wife, Chlothar tried pleading, writing that she was his very soul, and he could not live without her. Reading between the lines, Radegund shook her head, amazed at how gullible he must have thought she was.

A few years went by, and letters passed back and forth between the two with no result. Information drifted in through servants and friends that Chlothar had fathered a son called Gundovald on one of his concubines. Radegund prayed for the child and its mother, but was unmoved to return. Chlothar had raged that she should be jealous, that she should come back and do her duty to produce another legitimate heir. But Radegund wrote him calmly that he should be satisfied with the many sons he already had and require no more. Certainly, she wrote with a smile behind the words, if God had wanted a child to be born of her, Chlothar had given him every opportunity. Still Chlothar sent letters and messengers to her, demanding that she return, until she began to wonder if she were wrong in trying to escape the cross God had asked her to bear.

She fell asleep shivering and had a dream in which a holy anchorite called Dom John told her to give up all her worldly power. She remembered his name, and when she woke up and sent him a gift worth a thousand solidi, a piece of cloth woven with gold and studded with gems. Along with it, she sent a letter asking him to use his prophetic power to guide her. It was time, she thought, to officially end this unholy marriage which had battered her in body and soul.

Sitting at her writing desk the next morning, Radegund wrote the words that had come to her as she slept. "I will die before any king except my heavenly one unites with me. If compelled to return to the world, I will fast until my life ends. Pray for me." She sent these words to both the king and the anchorite who had advised her in her dream.

As if in answer to prayer, the next month Radegund had an unexpected visitor. She was kneeling in her courtyard, harvesting herbs and dropping them into a basket. The shadow of a man in a cloak fell over her, and she lifted her eyes. The man standing beside her was a priest, young and not very tall. She could hear his breath rasping in his throat and at once rose to seat him on a stone bench.

"You need water?" She asked him, frightened that the man might be dying.

"Nothing, thank you," the priest said, his frail shoulders shaking as he coughed. "My name is Gregory, my lady queen, and I come from Tours."

Radegund sat down beside him, sighing heavily. "I fear you come from my husband, the king, to tell me I must return to him. It won't do, you know. I was consecrated as a deaconess by Bishop Médard and will never go back to that marriage."

"You mistake me, my lady," Gregory said, snatching at breath between his words. "I come with good news. The bishop in Poitiers, has sent me to tell you that the king, your husband, has granted you freedom to pursue your vocation. King Chlothar is under orders from the great Bishop Germanus of Paris. Even Chlothar must bow to that saint. I am to take you to Poitiers myself."

"Why would such men care about me?" Radegund wrung her long, slender hands. It seemed to her impossible that Bishop Germanus had bothered with her letter to him. "How do I know this isn't some trick of Chlothar's to kidnap me?"

"I suppose you can't know. You'll have to trust me."

"Trust?" Radegund looked into Gregory's tired brown eyes, wrinkled at the corners with laugh lines, and tried to read through them into his soul. "You ask more of me than I can give."

"We must trust, my lady, or die," Gregory said. "Trust is all we have to give God. I think you know that, or you would not want to turn your life over to him as a nun."

Radegund was silent for a little while, looking deeply into her own heart, through the veils of grief and disappointment that swathed it. *Perhaps I am unwilling to let God take charge of my life. Here at Saïx, I am my own mistress, after all.* "In a convent, I would be in someone else's hands," she said, wishing she did not have to betray to this stranger the deepest fear she had.

Smiling, Gregory put his palms together and bowed his head. "We are always in someone else's hands, my lady. God's, I believe. I will go and rest now, if you will find me a bed. And please, some pillows to prop me up while I try to breathe."

This poor man trusts you, Lord, with his next breath and has come all the way here to guide me home. I must trust him or lean only on my own fearful self. Radegund guided Gregory to his room and promised him an answer in the morning. That night, she lay prostrate in front of the altar, wrestling with her desire to remain at Saïx, in charge of her own life, with no one making any demands upon her.

It came to her as she prayed that what her own prideful self wanted was a life disengaged from anyone else's expectations or demands, whether those of a husband or a bishop. Gregory was calling her to a life of discipline and service, she realized, and in that life, her choices would not be her own. Trembling, she felt her hands turn to fists on the cold stone floor. *What am I holding onto, Lord? Not my will, but yours be done.*

She fell into sleep, repeating these words over and over again. The next morning, she gathered her few possessions, closed up the estate at Saïx, and asked Leubovera to accompany her and Gregory to Poitiers. Glory pranced and tossed her head as she carried her mistress on the long Roman road to their new home. During the journey, Radegund became aware of the forests that had begun to encroach on old Roman farmlands. Here and there trees had burst through the pavement of the road and at times, the road ended altogether. Then the party had to ride among the trees, some of them taller than the farm buildings they had toppled as they grew.

Radegund reached out to touch one tall pine that might have lived in the ancient days when all of Francia had been forest. She imagined she could hear its deep, slow voice telling her that God had created near-timeless trees so that men might more keenly feel their own mortality. Perhaps it was not so strange that her people in the old days had sought spirit in the trees and longed to mingle their souls with it.

Radegund rode on, wishing she could build a hermitage for herself in a forest clearing, where the giant pines would be her only company. When their path curved back onto the road again, she sighed, knowing that the solitary life was not where God was calling her. *Your will, Lord Christ, not mine be done.* Taking deep breaths of the damp morning air, Radegund did not look back, but followed Gregory's lead into a life she could not control or predict. It would be as the priest said. She would have to trust that this time, God would bring her at last into his very self.

Everything depended, Radegund found, on Chlothar's will. By Frankish law, a woman could not embrace the religious life without her husband's permission. In consecrating her a deaconess, Bishop Médard had given her the status of a holy widow, dedicated to prayer, celibacy, and charity. That was the best he could do. The Council of Orleans in 533 had tried to keep women out of the clergy by downgrading the position of deaconesses so that they could not serve the church in any official way.

After all, women were by nature impure and should not touch any holy object or sacrament. They had to be veiled to take communion and could not touch the wafer as it was given to them. Radegund had wondered at these notions, since her husband was obviously much less pure than she, male as he certainly was. Her Lord had honored women and made them his friends, as she knew from reading the Holy Scriptures. *Why, then,* she asked herself, *did his priestly servants not do the same?*

It came to her all at once that Jesus had served even those who served him, washing the feet of sinful men who would betray him the next day. Women were called to follow Christ totally, for they had been graced with his desire to love and serve. Men, on the other hand, might do the best they could to follow the Lord, but God could not expect much of them. So Radegund mused as she rode next to Gregory. *Well, perhaps this man is an exception. He is too weak in body to do harm and too strong in spirit to intend it. I must let no other sort of man near me.*

Radegund spent the rest of the long journey dreaming of the joys that awaited her in the society of holy women. They would pray and sing and work together in harmony like the angels. Radegund would be the servant of them all, not a mother superior. If the City of God were to exist in this world, it would be composed of gentle women, giving alms, nursing the sick, and feeding the poor. No man could bend them to ugly purposes, for they were the brides of Christ, under the veil and behind a wall. As yet, she had no experience of convent life.

The loveliness of Poitiers swept her into ecstasy when she saw it for the first time. She and her party paused on the tall granite rocks above the city, and she took in a sweeping view of the place. Poitiers lay between the rivers Clain and Boivre, where it had grown up as a town rich with grain and commerce. Radegund could see the ancient baptistery of St. John, a low, stone hexagonal building that glowed as the morning sun lit the bright bits of pyrite in its surface. A stone bridge built by the Romans crossed both rivers and tall trees bowed above them. *It is a tranquil place,* Radegund thought, *a place where I can be alone with God in silence.*

Radegund's otherworldly thoughts came to an abrupt end when she arrived in Poitiers and found Chlothar awaiting her in the bishop's private rooms. He seemed larger and fiercer than ever, and the purple scar on his face almost glowed with pulsing blood. Sinking down on a bench beside the hearth fire, Radegund held one hand over her heart and closed her eyes, not wanting to see her husband, wanting only to erase him from her world like a bad dream. Gregory stood beside her, his hand on her shoulder.

"King Chlothar, Deaconess Radegund has come at the invitation of Bishop Germanus to begin her life as a nun here in Poitiers. I am Gregory, servant of the bishop and priest of Tours, your servant also." Gregory bowed to Chlothar, who looked at him with a vague benevolence, then turned back to Radegund.

"Do not fear, my lady, that I have any designs on you," Chlothar said, falling on his knees before his wife. "That saint, Germanus, has convinced me my soul's good depends on my letting you go."

"He has my thanks as do you, my lord." Radegund looked at the scarred, grizzled face before her, and felt a jolt of warmth burst through her body, as if she were a flower opening to light for the first time. This man who had done her such wrong was only the hand of God wiping away the dust from her soul. She leaned forward and cupped his face in her hands.

"Bless you, Chlothar, for your kindness to me. I'll pray for you every day of my life, that you may enter into the love of our blessed Lord." She looked at him more closely and saw the mark of the grave on this man. His skin was gray with imminent death, and his cheeks were cold. Pity melted her heart. An energy that she knew was not her own poured through her hands, warming them, and she felt for a moment that she was both lover and beloved.

"Radegund, I'm afraid to die without you." Tears filmed Chlothar's eyes, and his hands shook when they covered hers. "My soul's like black pitch, fit only for hellfire."

"My dear friend, you are no worse than the thief who died on a cross next to Our Lord and was assured of paradise because he repented. Open your heart to God. Love him as he loves you."

"Smile at me, Radegund," the king said turning his head so his one good eye could focus on her. "Give me your blessing and forgiveness."

"With my whole heart," she said, meaning it, to her own surprise. "After all, haven't you released me from our marriage? Given me the right to found a convent here in Poitiers? My cup is full and running over, Chlothar. You have my thanks and my forgiveness and my blessing, for whatever they're worth."

She smiled at him and then kissed him on the brow as if he were Christ, her beloved. For a moment, his ugly, ruined face became for her the luminous countenance of Jesus on the cross, sorrowful, yet full of a peace that passed understanding. *Thank you God for granting my deepest prayer, that I might love as you do, without conditions, without judgment, without expectations.* Her heart beat so hard she thought it might stop altogether and allow her to move the one step forward that would bring her home to heaven. *Forgive us our sins, as we forgive those who sin against us.* These words hit her soul like lightning firing a tree, so that she understood for a moment what it was to be God and to love as God loved.

"My lady, once my wife," Chlothar stammered, his voice hardly audible, "you've only to tell me what you want for this convent of yours, and I'll give it to you."

"Enough money to restore the estate outside the walls to a place where women can live cleanly and can serve the poor," Radegund said. "I trust you to provide for us, my lord, and we'll provide our prayers for you."

"You were ever the one to strike a hard bargain," Chlothar laughed. "I'll give you whatever you want, Radegund, soul of my soul, and count myself lucky for your prayers."

He was faithful to his promise, Radegund found as the months went on. When she needed money for rebuilding the ruined estate next to the city of Poitiers, Chlothar was quick to give it. As she had thought would happen, he died within the year, but left a large sum for the Abbey of the Holy Cross, Radegund's new foundation.

The convent's official life began at the time of his death, in 561. Its rule had been sent from St. Caesaria of Arles, and the saint had enjoined Radegund to be careful of letting men anywhere near her, "for you cannot fight lust if you do not flee from the presence of men," she wrote to the new foundress. Radegund smiled at that admonition and shook her head. *Chlothar cured me of any lust I might ever feel.* The new rule put the nuns to work copying manuscripts, reading prayers, doing needlework for the altar, tending the poor, and staying well away from the contamination of sex and power. Radegund agreed with what Caesaria had written her. She would keep men at a distance and make the City of God a garden of women only.

And so her foundation remained as a refuge for women over a period of five years. During this time, Radegund kept her connections open to the kings, especially Sigibert and Chilperic. She knew when Chilperic took new concubines; she knew when Sigibert planned to marry a virgin princess from Hispania. Despite St. Caesaria's rule that nuns never move from their sacred place, she felt called to leave her convent in 566 for the marriage of Sigibert and Brunhild, hoping that this union would be a rebirth of the peaceful, holy realm, a City of God in Francia.

At that wedding, she saved the life of the poet Fortunatus, not sure she should speak in his behalf, but feeling a tug at her heart like that Chlothar had caused when he asked her forgiveness. Why she cared for this foolish, prideful poet, she did not know, but she cared, and spoke for his life as if he had been her own brother.

When Fortunatus turned up at her abbey, Radegund was not sure what to do with him, once he had carried her message to Guntram. He was a man, after all, and subject to the weaknesses of Chlothar and the rest of them, careless of human feelings. He liked to drink and eat, she saw, and he was caught up in a childish, unmindful love for her. *Lord, what should I make of this poor fellow? Give me some hint as to what he might be good for.*

Fortunatus proved his practical worth by fixing the hypocaust network under the villa whenever a pipe burst, so that clean, warm water ran into the baths. Cleanliness was the one luxury Radegund insisted on, for both herself and her nuns. When Fortunatus came to her jubilantly announcing the repair of the baths, he was still damp and fresh from trying out his project for the first time. His black hair twisted in wet curls on his forehead, and his dark eyes danced.

For a moment, Radegund felt his energy pour over her, turning her alive and warm, so that she felt herself reaching for even more life. Her hands trembled as she imagined touching him. *He is beautiful, a beautiful man,* she thought. *Such a man would not have disgusted me as Chlothar did.* Then she shook her head and made the sign of the cross over her heart. *I have one Love,* she reminded herself, *the only one who never disappoints, never gives me pain, always carries me beyond my little self. Lord Jesus, be with me now.* As she said these words within herself, the image of Christ came forward in her mind, blotting out Fortunatus, and she no longer caught her breath at the sight of her friend.

"For once, a poet is worth something besides mere verses," Fortunatus said, with a bow to Agnes and Radegund, who sat at the kitchen table peeling turnips. "Ladies, your bath awaits, compliments of the poet in residence. I can't guarantee how long we will have water before another pipe cracks."

"I made candied dates for you," Agnes said shyly, handing her father a plate. "A trader from the south brought dates to our door, and I thought you might like them."

"And we have sweet apple juice for you, too," Radegund said, setting an ewer in front of him. She was pleased to see his smile as he reached for the drink. When Fortunatus smiled, his whole face lit up, white teeth shining against his tanned skin.

"What task will you set me next, Lady? I live to serve."

"I'm afraid you live to eat and drink, my friend," Radegund said, laughing. "Since I've vowed to fast for the sake of Chlothar's soul, I must find my pleasure in the appetite of others."

"You're right that I love food and drink," Fortunatus said, making the sign of the cross over the food. His mother had taught him that the sign must be made over so much as a piece of lettuce, for a demon might be sitting on it, hoping to be swallowed. The poet did not have the fear of demons that most people did, but made the sign anyway, just in case.

"God has given us the good things of the earth and shared his very being in bread and wine," he said. "Why shouldn't we be grateful?"

"I think our good Mother Radegund means that we must not see the things of this world as an end in themselves," Agnes said. "The Romans did that and so do the barbarians. Our path is different from theirs, I think." She looked at Radegund for confirmation.

"Each person must decide for himself what God wants of him," Radegund said. "For me, it is the way of sacrifice. For you, it may be something else. God will let you know, if you ask. It's true that this world, this life, is shot through with the glory of God, but we often stop halfway home to him."

"That's how it is with me," Fortunatus sighed. "I pray a little, but find more joy in making songs and eating your treats, Agnes. So much the worse for my soul."

"You are kind, though," Agnes said, "and surely no fasting or sacrifice is more important than that."

Fortunatus was about to answer when there was a crying out and slamming of doors that ended their conversation. Into the little kitchen hurtled a wild-eyed woman, screaming as if she had lost her wits. It took Radegund a moment to recognize the woman as Fredegund, Queen of Neustria. The queen's long pale blond hair was as tangled as a rat's nest and her clothes were ripped into rags. She howled as if the devil himself had entered her and threw herself on the floor in front of Radegund.

"My sons are dead," she cried, tearing at her own flesh until her throat bled. "They were carried off yesterday by the bloody flux. God took them in their innocent childhood, and left me alive to grieve them. Save me, holy Radegund. My sins have brought this trouble on me. Can there be any help for such a sinner as I am?"

Radegund stood up and held out her arms to the woman. "We're all sinners, Fredegund. Sometimes I wonder that God can love us, but be sure he does."

"Then why did he take my little boys?" Fredegund started to accept Radegund's embrace, then drew back, as if afraid to touch someone so good with her bloody hands.

Radegund sat down beside her on the floor, tears spilling from her eyes. No matter what she had heard of this woman, the loss of children was a weeping matter. She laid her hand on the woman's head, conscious of a dark, miasmic force roiling inside Fredegund, so strong that it seemed to spread the soil of the devil himself.

She remembered what Brunhild and Fortunatus had told her of the woman's past, and tried not to let the urge to judgment separate her from this sinner. *Have I not known temptation? Here is this woman, who killed to keep her man from straying, who killed to keep him in power. Is Fredegund's sin not simply different in degree from mine, not in kind?*

She thought of her insistence on keeping Fortunatus at the abbey, where she could see him whenever she wished, even if it meant his pain. *Lord, let me not judge my sister as a sinner, when I myself have kept the occasion of sin at hand, when I schemed to keep him near me by making his daughter my abbess.*

Fredegund is my sister in sin. Help me find words to comfort her. As she prayed, Radegund felt the Holy Spirit send its words through her.

"Your sons are with God," she said. "If you let Jesus love you as he loves them, you'll be with them, too. Can you do that, Fredegund?"

"I know only one kind of love," Fredegund said, in a low, gravelly voice, as if a man or a devil spoke through her. "And it doesn't have anything to do with God. In my life, I've learned you get what you need only by making people fear you. I love to make people fear me. It satisfies me, wrong or not."

"My poor dear," Radegund whispered, bending over the crumpled figure. *Fredegund*, she thought, *is more honest than most. She does not pretend a virtue that is not hers.*

"Any kind of love has to do with God, for God *is* love, the Holy Scriptures say. Go back to your husband and repent the evil you have done. God will hear your prayers, and mine for you. You will have another son, I promise. Give alms to the poor and love your people as a queen should. You will receive blessings for it."

When Fredegund at last stopped crying and left the abbey, Radegund was so exhausted that Agnes and Fortunatus had to carry her to her bed. Long after Fortunatus left them, frightened at seeing his queen so weak and tired, Agnes sat with Radegund, wiping her forehead with cool, wet cloths.

"Agnes, I wish I could retreat into an anchorite's cell," Radegund said. "Would God allow it, do you think?"

"How would we manage without you?" Agnes wrung out the cloth and soaked it in water again. "My poor father would weaken and go back to the world. I would fail to control Chlothild and her impossible nuns."

"Well then, I'll stay," Radegund sighed. "But I will be asking much of your father and you, Agnes. Pray for me. I feel dry as a winter leaf about to fall from the tree."

During the next months, Fortunatus worked on a poem about the ruin of Thuringia, telling Radegund's story as he had heard it from her lips. It became a very long, very grand poem, and when he brought it finally to Radegund for her approval, she read it in silence, not saying a word to the poet. The long poem was true, as poems go, but it did not tell the story of a heart broken by grief, or cruelty so harsh it killed all trust. *The words are elegant, the meter correct, but Fortunatus doesn't understand the depths of my despair,* Radegund thought, *since he has never touched those depths himself.*

When she had finished reading, Radegund put the pages aside, and looked for a long time out the window, where snow was falling so thickly the flakes blurred together into a white mist. She felt a heaviness that seemed to crush her bones. Putting her face in her hands, Radegund rested her elbows on the kitchen table.

"My dear lady," Fortunatus said, jumping to his feet. "Have my words disturbed you? I wanted only to honor your people and your past."

"I know what you intended."

Radegund let her tears fall as she remembered all the blood and death the poet had conjured up. "But I wish. . ."

"What kind of poem would serve you, my lady?" Fortunatus said, bending over her, trying to see her face.

"I think you might write something shorter," she said. "Something that would remind me of the kind of love God has given us in creation, when he comforts us with herbs and flowers and bread. I don't know, Fortunatus. You're the poet, not I, but I'd like to treasure something in this world before I go to the next."

Radegund was about to enter her hermitage to pray and fast for two months, in honor of Lent. Sometimes, when she went into her cell, she felt that she was going through a kind of death. As she prayed in her isolation, she felt she was being carried on a rising flame toward a silent fusion with the source and end of life. Her soul brimmed over with glory, and she became the flame that carried her God-ward in a blazing pentecost. At such moments she would not touch the food Agnes brought her or read the poems Fortunatus sent. Later, when she fell back into herself, Radegund took a little supper, arranged the flowers brought by her friends, and read the verses Fortunatus had brought to her door.

> *Radegund,* he wrote, *my thoughts will wander wide*
> *Searching everywhere for you.*
> *Your lamp burns far away, you have snatched it from our sight.*
> *Now all too heavy clouds shadow me without you here.*
> *A cave will shut you in, walling out all other life.*
> *We whom you lock outside, even more are jailed than you.*
> *Remember, runaway, not for long may you hide there.*
> *The months I spend without you pass slower than a year.*
> *You're stealing hours from me; God can see you any time.*
> *I feel they're all too brief, glimpses I have had of you.*
> *But in our prayers, we're joined, sharing in one common life,*
> *In thought I follow you where I'm not allowed to go.*
> *I pray that Easter joys will once more draw you safely home,*
> *And Easter light shine on us all with brightness twice its own.*

Radegund smiled and laid the page aside. Fortunatus had shown her his soul, and it was as it should be, ripe for God's love, though fixed on this world and her. *At least,* she thought, *the poem was short. It is his own soul the poet seeks, not me. Help him, Lord, to know the source and end of love, not only the bits and pieces lying in the dust of this world like dry, dead blossoms.*

She did not read the poem again, fearing it would feed her pride, but gave it to Agnes when the girl came to bring her a bowl of lentils and onions for supper. Poems were all very well, but Radegund preferred prayer that folded her like dough into a loaf swelling with life, feeding multitudes. She was leaving behind any special love for Fortunatus or Agnes, as her life force dwindled. All her children were Christ; all her love was his. She felt a blurring of separate things into one and a dissolving of her fear that nothing was to be trusted.

As the kingdom of Francia was broken by wars, Radegund's prayers penetrated the dark cloud hanging over her people and scored it with light. She could feel the muttering and moaning of her adopted countrymen as she lost herself in visions, travelling along radiant corridors of space, into the genesis and death of worlds unknown to her. Living in both time and eternity, Radegund burned with the pain of wars raging around her and melted in the love that carried the sorrowing world into the heart of God. Her prayers bore fruit, though not always in the way she had hoped.

Once more Fredegund came to the Abbey of the Holy Cross, this time bringing with her King Chilperic. Both were scowling at each other as if they had just had bitter words, but did not want to continue their fight in front of the holy woman. Radegund seated the two on either side of her, serving them grapes and cheese to put them in a better mood.

"There now, you can tell me what's wrong," Radegund ventured, when neither of her visitors volunteered to speak. "Chilperic, you've known me since you were a boy, and you were always ready to talk."

The king opened and closed his mouth a few times, like a fish gasping in air, but could not get any words out. His round red face, with its pinched little features, resembled a ripe melon about to burst. Radegund resisted the urge to pour a cup of water over his head to cool him down.

"My husband's friends have told him lies," Fredegund cried in her shrill voice, strained with fury and fear. "They say I've had an affair with Bishop Bertram of Bordeaux. Nothing is so evil that those nobles would not accuse me of it."

"But why come to me?" Radegund was more astonished at their presence in her home than at the accusation. She had, through Fortunatus, heard tales of the queen's affairs, but had paid no attention except to pray for the woman's soul.

"Because you can sense the truth," Chilperic finally choked out. "You can prophesy and see the future. I've seen you do it."

"My skills as a seer are much exaggerated," Radegund smiled. "Besides, I can't do that sort of thing unless God speaks to me. I can't make it happen."

Fredegund's face relaxed a little, and Radegund wondered if the woman were relieved that no mind-reading or sorcery would reveal her secrets.

"The nobles say I'm trying to kill my husband and set up Bishop Bertram as king. Have you ever heard such nonsense?"

Radegund, who had heard even worse nonsense than this from Chlothar, had no answer. Instead, she laid one hand over Chilperic's clenched fist. "Never mind what others say. What do you say, my son? Do you believe your wife would kill you when you have made her queen and fathered her children?"

"She has killed others who stood in her way," the king muttered.

"Only when enemies have stood in *our* way, have I killed," Fredegund cried, tears rising in her large brown eyes. When her eyes shone behind the mist of tears, she was even prettier than usual, and had doubtless used the effect more than once to win her way. "And I'd do it again!"

Remembering the fate of Princess Galswinth, Radegund shuddered slightly and put both hands in her lap, not wanting to touch either one of these demon-driven lovers.

"Go home to your daughter," she said, remembering that they still had one child living. "Together you have brought life into the world. Do not offend God, I beg you, by talk of killing this one or that. Instead, give alms to the poor children of Soissons. Build a hospice for the sick next to the cathedral. Work side by side to make your people glad of your rule. Will you do this?"

Chilperic met her eyes, but Fredegund looked down at her lap.

"We have much to repent," the king said in a low voice. "You have no idea how much."

"I'll do as you say, Radegund, but I repent only that I've failed to bring down Brunhild from her proud seat on Austrasia's throne, beside her son. The woman's pride galls me, and I haven't finished with her."

Fredegund raised her eyes and stared at Radegund as if daring the nun to argue the point. Repentance was clearly not on her mind.

Turning to Chilperic, who seemed a least a little sorry for his sins, Radegund raised her hand, half in blessing, half in warning.

"Many in Neustria are falsely imprisoned," she said. "Many of your officials have cheated the poor and harassed the innocent. Go home and undo the injustice done in your name, or your people will rise up in civil war. You wanted a prophecy. There, you have one. And here's another. You will soon have a son to fill the place of the ones who died."

She stood to end the interview. "Worry less about your wife, Chilperic, and more about your kingdom. God help you both."

In 584, not quite a year after his talk with Radegund, King Chilperic went on a hunting expedition. Twilight fell over field and forest so that he could not see well enough to go on with the hunt. Tired after his long day of riding, Chilperic dismounted from his horse, resting one hand on the shoulder of his servant. A stranger stepped forward and stabbed the king first in the armpit, then in the chest, opening wounds that soon brought Chilperic to an end.

Fredegund's four-month-old son, Chlothar II, was suddenly king of Neustria. The kingdom erupted in bloody reprisals by the oppressed against their oppressors. Estates were burned down. Wars broke out between rival cities.

If Fredegund had hoped to profit from her husband's death, which rumor said she had caused, she was disappointed. The Neustrian nobles had objected to Fredegund's effort to lift some taxes from the poor after she lost her two older sons to dysentery. She quickly reverted to her former ways, sending assassins to kill Brunhild and Childebert with poisoned daggers.

The assault failed when one of Fredegund's henchman was caught by Brunhild's guards and tortured into confession. Tired of her plots and scandals, the nobles of Neustria drove the widowed Fredegund into exile and took charge of her infant son Chlothar, now king. But even from a distance, Fredegund managed one last crime.

After a seven-year exile, Praetextatus had been reinstated as the Bishop of Rouen, where Fredegund was living, and crossed bitter words with her. He had not forgotten her cruelty to his godson Merovech and to him.

"You should mend your life," he said to her, "and turn your mind to higher things. You might then bring up your child in the peace of God."

Not saying a word, Fredegund swirled her skirts around her and swept off to plot her revenge. On the day of the Lord's Resurrection, when Bishop Praetextatus was saying Mass in the cathedral, an assassin hired by Fredegund stabbed him in the side. The bishop collapsed, holding onto the altar with one hand. He cried for help, but the clergy standing nearby didn't move, frightened as they were of Fredegund's retaliation. A few of his personal servants carried him to his chamber, where Fredegund had the gall to visit him on his deathbed. There Gregory attended him and heard his last confession, then listened in silent disbelief to the queen's hypocrisy.

"I can only hope," Fredegund said to the dying bishop, "that the man responsible for this deed will be caught and punished." Then she made the sign of the cross, piously rolling her eyes heavenward.

Bishop Praetextatus no longer had anything to fear from her. "We both know who has caused my death," he said, his voice for once firm and loud. "And God knows. You will feel his curse."

"Now, now, bishop, you can come to my house and my doctors will heal you," Fredegund said, her smile baring her pointed little teeth.

"It's my time to die," the bishop said, closing his eyes to blot her out of his sight. "My blood be on your head."

After hearing this story from Gregory, Radegund went silently to the abbey chapel, where she prayed for Fredegund's soul all through the night. The next day, not stopping to sleep, Radegund set Fortunatus to writing letters, first to King Guntram of Burgundy, and then to Brunhild and King Childebert.

Her worry, she explained to Fortunatus, was that the nobles who nurtured the infant king Chlothar II of Neustria would decide to fight Guntram and Childebert, one at a time, breaking the kingdom into small, warring counties and dukedoms, without any central government. The result, she feared, would be great suffering for the people of Francia.

"Do not allow the kingdom to be dismembered," she wrote to Guntram and Childebert: "If you two will make a binding alliance, the Neustrians will not dare to attack in young Chlothar's name." She urged Guntram to adopt Brunhild's son Childebert and to protect Queen Brunhild and her grandsons should Childebert die young. As she dictated the letters to Fortunatus, she closed her eyes and looked inward, at the larger landscape she had seen in her visions.

Sometimes, when she centered her soul in that place where the world ends and heaven begins, Radegund felt she could sense the future, however dimly. One scene she saw that made her breath catch, so that Fortunatus looked up at her in concern. Brunhild was old, white-haired, and being torn to pieces.

"Write a separate letter to Queen Brunhild, Fortunatus," Radegund said, when she could speak again. "Tell her that she can leave her son in charge of Austrasia, now that he is a man. She would do well to come here and live out her days in peace."

"Childebert is a strong-willed young fellow," Fortunatus objected. "Without his mother's influence, he will act the fool, like so many men in his family."

"That may be, but Brunhild has overstayed her time in power. She seems to feel she's invincible."

Fortunatus hung his head. "I gave her the ring of power when she grieved over Sigibert's death," he confessed. "Maybe she really is invincible now."

"Oh, that was not well done," Radegund said, in as close to a scolding as she had ever given her friend. "For a soul like Brunhild's, the ring is poison. You might better have thrown it in the river where it could do no harm."

"Do you see harm coming to the queen? I hope not." Fortunatus frowned until lines creased his forehead. She was surprised, since his face was usually smooth as a child's, unmarked by any sorrows. He was fond of Brunhild, Radegund knew, and she felt a moment's pang of jealousy. Then she laughed at herself for being as much a fool as any lovesick girl and put the thought aside.

Radegund went into her quiet space once more, closing out Fortunatus and the world around her while she prayed. Suddenly she had a lightning flash of vision, in which Duke Rauching and his Austrasian nobles joined forces with the boy king Chlothar's followers and destroyed Childebert in a bloody assassination, causing a war that could turn Francia into a smoking ruin.

"Write to Guntram, Fortunatus," she said, when she had come back to herself. "Tell him that Rauching plots against Childebert. Guntram must protect the boy. Hurry, and don't take time for fine words. I feel the plot has already gone far along."

The poet rode at a speed that exhausted even Glory, a horse that seemed to have the divine strength of the Valkyries' steeds. When he received the letter from Radegund, Guntram immediately warned his nephew of the plot, and wrote Brunhild as well, telling her that the hour of her vengeance against the vicious Duke Rauching was finally at hand.

Together, Brunhild and her son lured Rauching to the king's private chambers, first having sent soldiers to the Duke's various estates with orders to confiscate all his property. Childebert and Brunhild toyed with Rauching for a little while, not bringing up the matter of his treacherous alliance with Neustria, which they had confirmed by torturing the Duke's servants.

When Rauching was leaving the royal chamber, two burly soldiers grabbed him by the feet so that he fell to the floor and then hacked him to pieces. Brunhild watched him die and laughed to her son that the duke must be made of money, since gold coins and ornaments fell out of the fine clothes ripped from his body. His treasure was so large that people said he was richer than the king. But not for long. King Childebert took possession of all Duke Rauching's goods and properties, giving much to the church and to the Abbey of the Holy Cross, at Brunhild's command. After that time, Guntram and Childebert became the best of friends, encouraged by Radegund's efforts to bring them into an alliance.

In the summer of 587, Radegund took to her bed, weak and ill from her fasting. Ever since Rauching's death had been brought about by her letter, she had abstained from nearly all food, eating only enough to stay alive. She had the sense that her sacrifices were for the good of the kingdom and were not personal to her soul's welfare. *Every comfort I give up,* she felt, *strengthens the alliance between Austrasia and Burgundy.* Every prayer said as she struggled for breath was intended to save innocent lives.

She had fallen ill with a cold that turned into a gasping sickness reminding her of Gregory's asthma. In her efforts to breathe, she remembered the triumph of his soul over the pains of his body, and asked God to help her do the same. She thought of Christ on his Cross, of the relic in its tiny jeweled box that her friends had laid over her heart. *Lord Christ, my pain is nothing to yours. I pray you will use my suffering to relieve that of others. We are all one in you, members of one body.*

Agnes and Fortunatus sat beside her, praying for her recovery. Fortunatus read a poem he had written her to accompany the bouquet of violets she now held in her hands.

Had lilies whitened at this time of year,
Or had there been a delicate red rose,
Wild, or from my garden, I had picked them
And gladly sent the rich so poor a gift.
But since I lack all these, I'll choose elsewhere.
He offers roses who gives violets with love.
Yet in among these fragrant greens I send,
Richly blooms the violets' purple spray.
They breathe the royal purple that they wear.
Now grace, now fragrance, drenches all their leaves,
May what surrounds us all surround you too,
And on my fragrant gift be lasting bloom.

As he read, Fortunatus sniffed and wiped his eyes, turning his face away from Radegund. He looked to her like a very large, unhappy child, and she tried to lift her hand to touch his face. Her hand was too heavy, and she could not move it.

"What do you hear from Queen Brunhild?" she asked, wanting to distract him from his grief.

"She thanks you for your invitation to stay at the abbey," Agnes said, "but she's too busy with affairs of state."

"Please ask her again," Radegund's voice was so faint she could hardly hear it herself. "She will save herself much suffering if she comes to live here."

Agnes looked at her father and shook her head, tears sliding down her cheeks. "Dear mother, you must rest, not think of others."

"Not even of you?" Radegund smiled a little. "Agnes, you will join me in heaven soon. I know it. Now, my daughter, leave us alone. Fortunatus, I have something to say to you."

"Brunhild will not come," Radegund sighed, folding her hands over her heart, gathering the poet's violets close. "What a pity that she can't give up her power now. The time will come when she'll wish she had."

Fortunatus bent his head over hers to catch her words, so softly were they spoken. "I will urge her, Radegund. In your name."

"In the name of Our Lord," Radegund said. "Not of mine. If you can, my poet, I want you to become a priest after I die. What do you think of that?"

He sat back, rubbing his eyes. "Me? Who'd ordain such a fellow as I am?"

"Gregory would. Ask him. It's my dying wish for you that you follow Our Lord into his service. I fear that if you go back into the world, you will fall away."

"I fear you're right." Fortunatus took one of her hands and kissed it, as he had never dared to do during the twenty years of their friendship at the abbey. "I will do as you say, my sister, my friend. Pray for me always."

"Always." Radegund smiled once more, then took her last breath. Her face shone like a child's in sunshine.

Fortunatus thought that the face of Christ must have looked just this way, and could not grieve, as he thought he might, at her passing. She was with him, part of him, as she could not be in life. The poet took one of the violets and held it to his lips, thinking that Radegund and he were now twined together in Christ, two branches of one vine. He wanted to write a poem about it, but decided that for once wordlessness was the better part.

Two months later, in the Fall of 587, Guntram formally allied himself with Brunhild and Childebert II in the Treaty of Andelot. Brunhild was finally given the cities that had belonged to her sister, and Guntram adopted Childebert as his heir. Radegund had saved Francia from another civil war. To this day, the people of France pray at her tomb in Poitiers and remember her as Christ's peacemaker.

Epilogue
The Letter of Fortunatus

613 A.D.

I, Venantius Fortunatus, Bishop of Poitiers, servant of the Lord and of *Sanctissima* Radegund, that blessed queen who gave my soul its life in Christ, have this to report of the people who made the world I live in. Gregory died in 593 from his long illness and was acclaimed a saint by the populace of Tours, who loved him like the father he was to them. I was with him as he died and gave him absolution for his sins, though he seemed to me far too holy to need it. After my beloved Radegund's death, I became first a priest, then a bishop. Me, the drunken poet, the father of bastard children, God forgive me.

My gentle Agnes did not long survive her spiritual mother. I think she did not want to. Leubovera became abbess for a second time and had to fight the insurrection of Chlothild once again. This time, Gregory and I were able to keep the convent from collapse and the troublemakers were banished, snarling curses all the way to their place of exile. Radegund, I thank you for your help from heaven, since no one but you could have overcome the pride and hatred of that princess-nun. Chlothild was not the only one of the royals who kept Francia on the edge of chaos.

Fredegund never forgot an injury, nor did Brunhild. It is a miracle of God that the kingdom survived both these queens and their deadly quarrel. Gregory had not much good to say of either woman in his *Historia*, but I think he was too hard on Brunhild. The suffering she endured was greater than any she caused. The cruelest blow was not the manner of her death, but the loss of her son, Childebert, at the age of twenty-six.

After losing Childebert, Brunhild ruled relentlessly through her young grandsons, then her great-grandsons, to the fury of the nobles of Austrasia. Chlothar, Fredegund's son, slew all Brunhild's kin in 613, when the Austrasian nobles refused to defend her. They preferred Chlothar to Brunhild, since he was one of their own, a long-haired Meroving, no better than the worst of them.

Fredegund, that dreadful woman, died peacefully in her bed, after being exiled by her own son, Chlothar II, because he had been told she killed his father. Chilperic, her longsuffering husband, had been about to punish her for her sins against him, probably her scandalous affair with Bertram the Bishop, and heaven knows how many other men. God will judge her; I must not. Her crimes deserved hell, I think, but Radegund would have said we must look first at the log in our own eye before we inspect the dust mote in another's. If Radegund could forgive her husband, King Chlothar, I must forgive Fredegund. But it is hard to forgive her son.

The worst thing Chlothar II did, as he destroyed the descendents of Sigibert, was to make their great-grandmother, Brunhild, the focus of his hatred. I think Fredegund hung over her son like a succubus, egging him on into a cruelty beyond belief. What happened was this. My soul pains me to remember, and I will not make much of the story.

I was called to Brunhild at the end of her life, after she had been tortured for three days by King Chlothar's henchmen. She had asked for me in her anguish, wanting me to give her absolution. So I was with Brunhild when she lay on her pallet in prison, waiting for execution.

The nobles she had offended in her grasping for power had finally turned on the foreign queen, driving her out of Austrasia, into Burgundy. Her answer was to set her younger grandson, Theodoric, against his illegitimate older brother, the king of Austrasia. Theodoric killed his brother and promptly died himself. Brunhild, undeterred by these warnings of divine Providence, insisted on trying to rule the kingdom in the name of her infant great-grandsons. By then, the nobles of Austrasia had had enough of her. They called in King Chlothar II of Neustria to end Brunhild's reign and her efforts to create a central government in the imperial Roman style, a closed circle of absolute power. They killed her great-grandsons in front of her, then put her on the rack.

"Who would have thought, poet," she said, holding her sore sides as she took painful breaths, "who would have thought that the Queen of Austrasia would break and die at the hands of Fredegund's son?"

"I'm here to confess you, lady." I bowed my head and closed my eyes, unwilling to see her bruises and burnt skin. "Not to speak about the sins of others." I prayed to the Blessed Radegund in heaven to intercede for this wreck of a woman. Then I gently touched the queen's brow and her heart with the sacred relic of the Holy Cross, borrowed from Radegund's tomb. "Open your heart to God. Ask pardon for your sins, and you will be forgiven. So Our Lord has promised."

"Then hear me." Brunhild spoke in a voice that seemed like a thunderclap, sharp and final. "I have sinned in my pride and bargained with God. My lineage has failed. Fredegund has won and her son will rule. May God have mercy on me for this hellish pride that has undone me and all the ones I loved."

"The larger scene is not yet clear, my lady. Do not despair."

The queen pulled off the ring of Pythagoras. "When I read the inscription, I understood why, at the end, the powerful of this world always despair. Do you know, poet, what the inscription says?"

I shook my head. "I never found anyone who could read it."

"I'll tell you, since the first language I read as a child was written in the runes of my northern ancestors. The words mean this: 'Might may triumph over truth, but truth laughs last.'

"A fitting epitaph for kings and queens, my lady. Should it be yours?"

Brunhild gave me a tired smile, and said, "Whatever is to come, I must put away my pride and give up all I thought to win. Here, poet, take back your cursed ring. It brought no luck to me or my family. My only trust now is in Christ's love. I can hear him calling me even now, and his voice is music."

"If it brought wisdom at the end, the ring has done its work. God will surely hear your prayer," I said, putting the ring of Pythagoras into the pouch that hung from my belt. "And God will take you home." I sang the Our Father for her, and she gripped my hand as if she could feel the song move from my body to hers along inaudible pathways. She had communion from me, and I gave her absolution.

Poor, poor old woman. The next day Chlothar's men stripped her naked and tied her to a wild horse. It dragged her across rocky ground until bits of her body were strewn everywhere, to feed wild dogs and carrion birds. I found a piece of her flesh, wrapped it in an altar cloth as if it were a relic, and took it home with me for burial in holy ground.

The ring of Pythagoras I carried to the place where the river Seine flows deepest. Winter winds swayed the naked beech trees lining the water, so that they bowed and mourned like women at a grave. I could almost hear their song, as the bare, icy branches shook and muttered in the snow-laden wind. My hands were cold and stiff, for I am now an old man, unfit for night riding in winter. Pausing to watch the full moon roll through the swirling gray clouds, I looked at the ring a last time, praying that God would bring it to the hand of some wise being in a later age, when men did not behave worse than wild beasts.

In my own time, such a ring could bring only sorrow, for wisdom and mercy are now in short supply. I kissed the ring, in honor of Pythagoras and Boëthius and all the noble souls who had worn it, gifting the world with their strength and goodness. Then I threw it into the river, watching as its diamond caught fire in the moonlight. The ring seemed to glow as it sank under the water and was extinguished like a drowned ember.

To remind myself that the ring had not been my only inheritance, I touched Radegund's rough cross that she had given me on her deathbed, and the rich sound of a hundred notes, all in harmony, sang within me, as if God had suddenly opened heaven to my ears. No loss, I thought, only change. Only a spiraling upward into new forms. In them, the best of the old order of things would be transfigured by the music of light, to be sung by the saints of God, on earth and in heaven.

The next day I went to the grave of my beloved Radegund in Poitiers, I asked the convent sexton to dig a grave next to Radegund's and laid Brunhild's remains in it, saying the Church's prayers for the dead. *Rest in peace, poor ruined queen. May light perpetual shine upon you.* In a way, she had come home, as Radegund wished her to. Soon, soon, I will join them in the garden that is the heart of Christ, where the music of angels never ends, and we will all be gone into the world of light. Amen.

> We are seemingly between two epochs: the dying Sensate culture of our magnificent yesterday and the coming Ideational [spiritual] culture of the creative tomorrow... The light is fading, and in the deepening shadows it becomes more and more difficult to see. The night of the transitory period begins to loom before us, with its nightmares, frightening shadows, and heart-rending horrors. Beyond it, however, the dawn of a new great Ideational culture is waiting to greet the men of the future.
>
> Pitirim Sorokin, *Social and Cultural Dynamics* (NY, 1937, v. III), p. 535

Historical Afterword

Before Christianity was introduced in northern Europe, a rich pagan mythology existed, into which the story of Sigibert and Brunhild was later interwoven. The legend of the ring, which the Siegfried of legend wrested from otherworldly powers and gave to Brunhild, carried the energy of ancient, pre-Christian culture into the love story of an ill-fated hero and a semi-divine woman. In *The Niebelungenlied*, a thirteenth-century epic poem, Siegfried lost his memory of Brunhild and loved another woman instead. Brunhild's rage brought Siegfried's death upon him, and she threw the ring of power into the Rhine River. She then rode into the fire that burned Siegfried's body. So died the royal lovers, as had the new Roman Empire that their originals, Sigibert and Brunhild, hoped to build. Their efforts may have been largely futile, but some good came of them.

Springing out of Roman ashes, the new nation-state of France was shaped by both religious law and a belief in the God-granted right and responsibility of rulers. These kings and chieftains owed their power to warlords, not to an emperor, and the warlords lost few opportunities to remind them of it. From their Germanic tribal past, the Franks kept a fundamental belief in the rights of the nobles who made and unmade kings, as the Senate of old republican Rome made and unmade emperors.

Unlike the rulers of Rome, however, the Merovingian kings of Gaul were not deities, although they were said to have god-like powers to heal the sick. Merovingian kings, with their long hair and lecherous habits, were the celebrities of their time. As is the case with the rich and famous in our own day, most of their excesses raged unchecked. Still, a political, religious poet like Fortunatus and a saint like Radegund could chide kings guilty of atrocities into obeying the spiritual laws of bishops. King Guntram of Burgundy, a patron of Fortunatus, was regarded by the people of his time as a saint, since after all, he had murdered only a few people. Such was the state to which society in France had fallen.

What had begun in the first century after Christ as a persecuted minority faith held by slaves and tradesmen had morphed by the early fourth century into the favored state religion under Constantine. As the political power of the imperial church increased, hermits and monks developed the contemplative, spiritual aspect of the new religion. The church was now committed to forming the conscience of the state, to supplying educated administrators for bishoprics, and consolidating its power among the newly converted barbarians, such violent people that the idea of a gentle Christ dying on the Cross disturbed their warrior sensibilities. "If my men and I had been there," King Clovis boasted on hearing of the Crucifixion, "We would have saved him and slain the Romans."

He rather missed the point, having no idea of what the point of self-surrender was. The bishops and priests had all they could do to restrain the cruelty of the new warrior-rulers, which they did with canon law and rituals that blended pagan and Christian forms of worship. The great emphasis of the Roman Church on literal and ritual aspects of religion is understandable in light of the barbarian challenge faced by her leaders after the death of imperial Rome. Fundamentalism and conservatism in religious matters largely replaced the philosophic speculation of the early church, though Arianism and Monophysitism remained to set Christians battling each other to the death over the nature of the Christ who taught, above all, love.

The Arianism of the Goths was tinged with the Neoplatonism of eastern, urban Christianity that like Judaism viewed God as utterly other and alone. Being incarnate, Christ could not be seen as God by an Arian, but only an intermediary between flesh and pure spirit. Perhaps this vision of the Arians smoothed the way for the Muslim conquest that would soon come, since the two faiths had in common the immutable, unfleshed mystery of God, with Christ as his prophet, not his other Self.

For the Greek Monophysites, Christ was so much God that he was not man. Empress Theodora's Monophysite belief was taken up by Emperor Justinian, much to the consternation of his western subjects. The incarnational creed of Athanasius, on the other hand, attracted ascetic monks and western Romans who were neither in the Byzantine orbit nor steeped in Greek literary culture. The important issue for them was to abandon the old secular society for a new spiritual order, living the life of the spirit while still in the body. To become a holy man or woman, separate from entanglements with the pagan past, meant embracing the desert, not the city. The incarnate Christ of Athanasian orthodoxy was the model for the inner-directed holy hermit like St. Anthony of Egypt and later for St. Benedict and the European religious communities like Radegund's that were influenced by him.

Hermits and monastics were the ones who tended the flame of spirituality that had created the Christian religion in the first place. The currents of Gnosticism, mysticism, and esotericism that flowed through the depths of Western Christendom was split off from the executive branch of a Western Church that had little time for the inner life, what with Huns, Goths, and later Vikings burning and pillaging churches almost as fast as churches could be built.

From that time to this, mystics have been suspect by ecclesiastical authorities, even as Jesus himself was feared by the priests of his day for his insistence on spirit being above law. The Manicheans that influenced St. Augustine's rigorous piety saw the physical world as defective and cut off from the world of spirit. For them and for those Christians who were touched by their dualistic message, the world and the flesh were suspect. Given the picture of both world and flesh drawn by sixth-century historian Gregory of Tours in his *History of the Franks*, it is not surprising that hermits and monastics opted for a life untainted by power, riches and sex.

Meanwhile, priests and bishops consolidated temporal laws, basing them on Christian and pagan sources. Under the ground of diocesan and state religion grew the seed of spiritual practice and good works. From these origins would ultimately flower Chartres Cathedral, the University of Paris, hospitals, bank-funded commerce, the art of Giotto and the social revolution of St. Francis. But it would have taken a great leap of faith on the part of sixth-century people to see their murderous, ignorant, and bleak century as the birth-time of radical and world-shaping innovation.

For us, such a leap is not so hard, since our age is no holier than theirs and no less hard-pressed by savagery and greed. But we, too, live in a time when faith is being reborn and saints living around us quietly shed the light of God on all creation. Like people in every age, we have the choice to grow in sacred ground or merely live as troubled guests on the dark earth.

Historical Events

Events and characters in *The Ring and the Cross* are real, except for Gertrudis and Phoebe. Given the wayward temperament of the young poet, celibacy in his youth seems unlikely. We do not know who the father of Agnes was. The story of the Ring is drawn from the *Volsung Saga* and *The Niebelungenlied,* but the Ring's connection with Thor and Pythagoras is imaginary. Most of the details in the novel are drawn from the *History of the Franks*, by St. Gregory of Tours.

531	Thuringia is conquered by King Chlothar I; Radegund is taken to Francia
539	Radegund marries Chlothar, leaves him after 8 years
561	Radegund founds Abbey of the Holy Cross in Poitiers
566	Sigibert and Brunhild marry in Metz; Venantius Fortunatus comes to Francia
566	Galswinth is murdered by Fredegund
567	King Charibert dies childless, leaving Tours and Poitiers to Sigibert
569	Revolt at Holy Cross Abbey. Radegund and Abbess Leubovera vs. Chlothild; Fortunatus comes to live at the Holy Cross Abbey
573	Gregory becomes Bishop of Tours
575	Sigibert assassinated by Fredegund at Vitry near Tournai; Chilperic captures Paris and Soissons, and banishes Brunhild to Rouen
584	Chilperic dies
587	Radegund dies in August; Treaty of Andelot in September makes peace among the Merovingian rulers
593	Guntram of Burgundy dies
594	Fredegund dies
612-13	Brunhild dies with all her kin. Fredegund's son Chlothar II (d. 629) becomes King of Francia. Fredegund's grandson Dagobert (d. 639) is the last functioning Merovingian king. That dynasty is replaced by Pippin, Mayor of the Palace, and his Carolingian line. Muhammed begins his public ministry in Mecca.
632	Muhammed's armies begin their sweep of North Africa, the Middle East, and Spain, stopped by Charles Martel, ancestor of Charlemagne, at Tours in 732.

Select Bibliography

Baudonivia, Vita S. Radegundis, MG, ed. B. Krusch.

Brown, Peter, *The Rise of Western Christendom*,

_____, *The World of Late Antiquity*, W. W. Norton: New York, 1971.

Cameron, Averil, *The Later Roman Empire*, Harvard University, Cambridge, MA, 1993.

Fortunatus, Venantius, *Personal and Political Poems*, Trans. Judith George, Liverpool University Press, Liverpool, 1995.

_____, *Vita S. Radegundis Reginae*, MGH, ed. B. Krusch.

Geary, Patrick J., *Before France and Germany*, Oxford, NY, 1988.

George, Judith, *Venantius Fortunatus*, Oxford University Press: Oxford, 1992.

Gregory of Tours, *The History of the Franks*, trans. Lewis Thorpe, Penguin: London, 1974.

Rogers, Barbara, *Venantius Fortunatus: A Translation*, Unpublished Dissertation, Rutgers University: New Brunswick, NJ, 1971.

_____, "Siegfried and Brunhilde: The Politics of Mythic Transformation," *Mythosphere: A Journal for Image, Myth, and Symbol*, v. 1, issue 4, pp. 523-540.

Rosen, William, *Justinian's Flea: The First Great Plague and the End of the Roman Empire*, Viking Penguin: New York, 2007

Smith, Julia M. H. *Europe After Rome*, Oxford University Press, Oxford, 2005.

Thierry, Augustin, *Tales of the Early Franks*, trans. M.F.O. Jenkins, University of Alabama Press, Alabama, 1977.

Wemple, Suzanne Fonay, *Women in Frankish Society: Marriage and the Cloister*, University of Pennsylvania Press, Philadelphia, 1981.

Questions for Study Groups

The two symbols, Ring and Cross, represent two different world views. How would you describe each one? How are they apparent in our own time?

1.   In what ways does *Romanitas* fail Boëthius in his last hours? Why do you think the ideals and institutions of Rome, as described in the novel, were unable to survive the economic and social collapse of the empire?

2.   In what ways does our own culture, also an imperial one, resemble what you know of the late Roman Empire? How are we different?

3.   Assimilating an immigrant population creates stress on a society. What stresses do you observe in sixth-century France that remind you of our own immigration problems? What solutions might Christianity offer that would make assimilation less painful?

4.   If you were one of the Frankish invaders, what might your attitude be toward the Roman culture you saw breaking down around you? What resentments, fears, and attitudes might mark your feelings toward the Gallo-Romans you were displacing?

5.   If you were one of the civilized old aristocracy, like Boëthius, Fortunatus, and Gregory, how might you have felt toward the new ruling class of northern invaders? How would their unfamiliar behavior affect your own way of life? (Hint—try looking at some of the new kinds of religious views of Buddhism and Islam Hispanics and their impact on American religious thought. What are their positive and negative aspects? You might look at such topics as moral behavior, spiritual seeking, and an exclusive belief system.

6. The breakdown of Roman socio-political order caused some new trends: barter instead of a cash economy, confiscatory taxes, government according to "might makes right," currency inflation, the breakdown of social services, pervasive violence, and the debasement of language and culture. How does our own society reflect similar trends? How does it differ from Rome in the time of collapse?

7. The Christian faith has been blamed for the fall of Rome. How does *The Ring and the Cross* counter such an opinion? Where do you think the blame lies for the failure of a society to flourish or for its demise?

8. Each of the four central characters—Boëthius, Fortunatus, Brunhild, and Radegund—has a different idea of how to live a Christian life. Create a discussion among these four on the subject of 'Christian Responsibility to Society,' and another discussion on what, specifically, Christians can do individually or collectively, to bring peace and justice to the world?

9. What people of our own time are similar to the four central characters of the novel? Look at contemporary sages, artists, statesmen, and holy people, comparing them and their actions to the lives of the four central characters of *The Ring and the Cross*.

10. Many Christians believe the End Times are imminent, as they did at the time of Rome's fall. How might such a belief shape social and individual behavior? For instance, Brunhild believed that only a return to old Roman order and standards could save Europe. Can we preserve the best of the past and go on to a new and different future? Based on the words of Christ in the Bible, how do you think he would answer this question?

MOON BLUE

The poignant story of a battle-fatigued WW II hero's homecoming.

Sgt. Rollins is a young white southerner with a Medal of Honor in his pocket, a load of shrapnel in his back, and a mission to find the missing granddaughter of the Black woman who raised him. Before solving a murder case, he falls in love and finds himself in more danger than on the battlefield of Guadalcanal.

$9.95 U.S.
$10.95 Canada
078-0-9834956-1-1

 SpiritBooks

Also from SpiritBooks

Yeshua's Dog:
A Gospel Love Story
by Barbara Rogers
Illustrated by Tamaris Johnson

When a dog decides to follow Jesus Christ through his ministry in ancient Israel, we see what real devotion looks like. Human followers doubt and betray the Master, but his dog is there for him until the end, sharing his sorrows and his joys.

Yeshua's Dog is a reverent and vivid re-telling of the Gospel story, one which will inspire readers of all ages.

$9.95 U.S.
$9.50 Canada
ISBN 978-0-9834956-0-4

www.ingramcontent.com/pod-product-compliance
Lightning Source LLC
Chambersburg PA
CBHW051157290426

44109CB00022B/2492